Sustainable Development for Public Administration

Sustainable Development for Public Administration

Deniz Zeynep Leuenberger
John R. Bartle

M.E.Sharpe
Armonk, New York
London, England

Library of Congress Cataloging-in-Publication Data

Leuenberger, Deniz Zeynep.
 Sustainable development for public administration / by Deniz Zeynep Leuenberger and
John R. Bartle.
   p. cm.
 Includes bibliographical references and index.
 ISBN 978-0-7656-2272-3 (cloth : alk. paper)—ISBN 978-0-7656-2273-0 (cloth : alk. paper)
 1. Political planning—Environmental aspects. 2. Policy sciences. 3. Public administration —
Environmental aspects. 4. Sustainable development—Political aspects. 5. Nonprofit
organizations—Management—Environmental aspects. I. Bartle, John R., 1958– II. Title.

JF1525.P6L48 2009
351.01—dc22   2009002562

We dedicate this book to our spouses, Derek Leuenberger and Lori Elliott-Bartle, with love and admiration, and to our children, Kelsey and Jocelyn Leuenberger and Alex and Sarah Bartle, in the hopes that their world will be safe, fair, and sustainable.

—DZL and JRB

Contents

List of Exhibits

Sustainable Development for Public Administration

1

Focus on Sustainability

A New Direction for Public Administration

"Sustainability," "environmental sustainability," and "sustainable development" are becoming increasingly important concepts in public administration. With increasing demand on resources, governments, civil society, and organizations all over the world are focusing their attention and energies on managing the impact of humans on their environments, integrating environmental sustainability and sustainable development while still preserving the welfare of citizens. This is, of course, not an easy charge. The complex work of the public administrator balances citizen equity, responsiveness, effectiveness, efficiency, and, now, sustainability in day-to-day practice and planning.

As public organizations adopt environmental sustainability as a tenet of good practice and theory, certain questions arise. Why is environmental sustainability important to public administration? What is the role of public administrators in planning and implementing sustainable development within agencies and communities? Few people would argue about the connection between sustainability and efficiency and reduction in waste. All agencies and communities benefit from increased efficiency and reduced waste as long as other tenets, such as participation and equity, are not compromised. Environmental sustainability moves beyond economic efficiency and incorporates these other tenets of public administration as well. Further, sustainable development requires the cooperation of professionals and experts from a variety of practices and disciplines. In public administration, professionals with backgrounds in community development, economics, psychology, education, ecology, sociology, transportation, engineering, geography, and many other fields work together. Public administration includes practitioners from local, state, federal, and international public and nonprofit organizations. Not only are environmental sustainability and sustainable development therefore, philosophically matched with the tenets of public administration, but the multidisciplinary nature of public administration provides the perfect opportunity to foster an environment wherein sustainable development can be meaningfully applied to community decision-making and practice. Public administrators, as translators and collaborators, may be able to facilitate communication on environmental sustainability and promote meaningful change in communities.

In order to discuss environmental sustainability and sustainable development, a definition of the terms is a helpful beginning. Environmental sustainability is a philosophy that requires the use of natural resources in such a manner that their quantity does not diminish over time or across generations. Environmentally sustainable systems rely on tools and approaches such as renewable resources, reduced consumption, technological advancements, and managerial efficiency to maintain resources at their current level or higher levels. Citizens of the future, under environmental sustainability, should enjoy resources and welfare at about the same level as people do today. Environmental sustainability also offers the potential for citizens to enjoy an increase in resources and welfare in the future. Although "sustainability" has increasingly been used to mean environmental sustainability, it is also defined as long-term success or preservation of organizations, organizational plans, or economic prosperity that may not have an environmental or natural capital dimension. This book will focus on sustainability issues that are rooted in the management of natural resources or capital.

Sustainable development is a plan of action that integrates environmental sustainability into decision-making. This type of planning suggests that any discussion of growth, development, and consumption should include steps to approach environmental sustainability as closely as possible. A completely sustainable system may not be possible in practice, but planners should attempt to make processes as efficient and effective as possible, providing goods and services with the lowest negative impact on the environment. Environmental sustainability and sustainable development depend on the consideration of short-run and long-run consequences of human action on human and environmental welfare.

Environmental resources are a form of capital, often called natural capital (Hawken, Lovins, and Lovins 1999). In general, capital is a stock of a resource; that is, an accumulated value based on previous investments *elaborate on "weak susty"*

minus depreciation or use. Other forms of capital include human capital, physical capital, and financial capital. Human capital is the stock of human resources accumulated through education, training, and experience. Physical capital is the value of machines, equipment, and structures. Financial capital is financial wealth in the form of stocks, bonds, cash, and other financial instruments. A definition of "weak sustainability" is an increasing value of total capital (Rogers, Jalal, and Boyd 2006; Pearce, Markandya, and Barbier 1989). Limited though this definition may be, it helps illustrate the interaction between these types of capital. This viewpoint would see sustainability enhanced if trees were harvested to produce financial capital of greater value, or if government spending on highways were shifted to spending on workforce training if the value of the latter were higher. Environmental sustainability and sustainable development are closely linked with tenets or canons held in high respect within public administration. In fact, sustainable development focuses on three tenets of public administration: efficiency, equity, and participation (Leuenberger 2006; Svara and Brunet 2004). One particular model of sustainable development, called broad-based sustainable development, stresses the tenets of healthy economy, equity, sustainability, and participation (Weaver, Rock, and Kusterer 1997). Public administration and sustainable development share many foundational themes, facilitating the application of sustainable development to decision-making in public and nonprofit organizations (Bartle and Leuenberger 2006). Sustainability is not just an environmental perspective, but also rather a holistic approach that is consistent with the founding values of public administration and naturally extends it to the challenges of the future. This type of planning is taking a hold in organizations that are local, state, federal, and international in scope. Organizations that provide transportation, environmental protection, health and human services, education, and economic and community planning are embracing sustainable development across the world.

Planning requires the setting of goals and the measurement of outcomes. Models of sustainable development concentrate on three types of goals setting. Goals are rooted in biological, economic, and social systems (Barbier 1987). In looking at biological systems, administrators would consider the impact of organizational decisions and actions on genetic diversity, species resilience, and biological productivity. For example, in building a dam, the planners would consider impacts on local fish, insects, plants, and mammals, their ability to reproduce, their availability as a food source for other species, and the impact of the ecological changes on human biology. Efficiency, equity in distribution, and social welfare improvements are the focus of economic goals. Economic goals encourage reduction of waste and duplication, balance of costs and revenues, long-run financial welfare for citizens, and fair distribution of gains from the use, production, and sale of natural resources. Social system goals include citizen participation and social justice as major components of agency decision-making and planning. Respect for the beliefs of indigenous peoples, the incorporation of knowledge held by citizens regarding their communities, gender equity, and assurance of fair and democratic citizen participation in agency planning are examples.

Environmental sustainability and sustainable development are theoretical approaches to managing real-world problems. Both are gaining importance as public administrators learn to manage finite and increasingly scarce natural resources. Subsequent chapters of this book will introduce the application of sustainable development, its theoretical and foundational roots, and its measurement and evaluation.

Local to Global Impacts of Sustainable Planning

Sustainable development is both a local and a global issue and, for that matter, an issue for any level of government between the two. Decisions of individuals at local levels and at the global level are in constant interaction with each other. For example, coal consumption by citizens in a local village in China affects air quality not only in that village, but also across the nation and across the world. Similarly, carbon dioxide emissions from cars in every town and every city in the United States have impacts on climate change around the world. Some of the solutions to problems of environmental management can be handled at the microlevel and some solutions require macrolevel planning; many require both types of consideration. Microlevel solutions focus on small units of analysis in decision-making, such as an individual citizen or organization. Macrolevel solutions attempt to take a wider view of the decision-making arena, perhaps focusing on analysis of a nation, a group of nations, or a large physical region. Regardless of whether a public administrator works in a local, state, federal, or international organization, sustainable development should and can be a part of agency planning and management. In fact, most complex environmental problems today require a great deal of collaboration at all levels of government, as well as partnership between governments, nonprofit and nongovernmental organizations, international organizations, citizens, and businesses.

Sociologist George Ritzer, in his popular book *The McDonaldization of Society* (2008), suggests that organizations in the United States have developed a bureaucratic system of service provision and customer management that has influenced organizational process and decision-making across the world. He suggests that control, efficiency, predictability, and calculability are primary tenets of this type of organization, the foundations of which are closely related to division of labor and the assembly line. Human beings are treated as part of a machine and the organization easily replaces individuals who are not living up to expectations.

Essentially, Ritzer argues that organizations are adopting practices based on the development of the fast-food industry in the United States. The goal of such organizations is to process goods and services in a manner that maximizes outputs and reduces costs while leading citizens through the system as quickly as possible. The advantage is that many citizens can receive needed goods and services at potentially low costs. Unfortunately, it is difficult to address a citizen's unusual or unexpected request under this system. One of the reasons that organizations with complex service delivery systems may not be as efficient as a product-providing organization is that they must take the time to assess the needs and wants of each citizen in the queue. The line at the Department of Motor Vehicles can be more efficient than the provision of child protective services because citizens receiving driver's licenses have very similar needs that can be addressed quickly without in-depth analysis, while families must be assessed for a number of strengths and weaknesses before being provided services through social service agencies.

In addition to problems with citizen responsiveness, systems focused on the type of efficiency discussed above may not calculate the costs on natural capital or resources drawn from nature. Goods and services may be priced too low because of this exclusion, encouraging overconsumption. One of the problems with the expansion of the Western style of capitalism and economic development is that it has not fully incorporated the costs of business

---

Coming to Terms
Sustainable Development and Smart Growth

Sustainable development and smart growth share a focus on long-term planning and management of multiple community systems. Smart growth is a theory of urban planning that addresses urban sprawl by emphasizing mixed-use development, public transportation systems, and growth in city centers. Although smart growth and sustainable development may go hand in hand in development of environmental sustainability, they are distinct concepts. Sustainable development is planning that may be used to balance human and environmental needs in any level of public or nonprofit agency and the communities they serve. Sustainable development is a tool for managing community capital in a manner that seeks to achieve this balance by preserving the value of capital in the long run, which may include choosing not to develop or initiate growth in communities.

to the environments. Globalization of consumerism and consumption has the potential to tax world resources beyond repair. For instance, if automobile ownership in China were to approach per capita rates of ownership in the United States, the impact on air quality, oil resources, and global climate change would be devastating to the environment. In order to create workable solutions to the world's problems, public administrators and nonprofit managers must consider the impact of economic and social globalization on humans and their environments, bearing in mind the special characteristics of environments and their people.

Systems Theory, Risks, Partnerships, and Outcomes

Governments and nonprofit organizations have an enormous role to play in environmental sustainability. Governments are in the business of managing risk, and nonprofit organizations fill in gaps in risk reduction that governments are not able to address (Giddens 2003). Risks require humans to use rational decision-making to avoid losses and improve gains in the future (Giddens 2003). Modern societies are able to envision solutions to the problems of risk not only for short-term gains, but also for long-term gains. Jared Diamond's book *Collapse: How Societies Choose to Fail or Succeed* (2004) suggests that societies must eliminate decision-making that places long-run environmental resources at risk. Environmental resources are at risk when humans are unable to adapt their behavior in favor of more sustainable practices because of social beliefs and training. If the future is seen as a territory to be colonized instead of as a space to be preserved, if societies rely on undiscovered or undeveloped technologies instead of revising current behavior, if behavioral changes are seen as too costly in the short run, if costs to future generations are ignored, and if societies fail to let go of economic and consumption practices that have huge, long-term, negative consequences, then societies may not be able to survive the long-run limitations of resources, thus reaching the carrying capacity of the planet (Giddens 2003). If societies are unable to address environmental limitations privately, then government intervenes. This intervention, addressing market failures such as lack of competition, externalities, inequities in resource distribution, and dissemination of information and knowledge, may take the form of regulation, taxation, education, and subsidies (Anderson 2003). Nonprofit organizations contribute by focusing their resources on citizen education, environmental advocacy, and championing of human rights.

How do public administrators make good decisions about environmental planning? Time and place knowledge and scientific knowledge are critical components of sound environmental decision-making (Ostrom, Schroeder, and

Marine Debris Tracker

Wynne 1993; von Hayek 1945). Both types of information are mandated in "any effort to develop infrastructure that can be sustained over a long period" (Ostrom, Schroeder, and Wynne 1993). Time and place knowledge is gained through the intimate contact of citizen experts with their environments. For instance, individuals tend to have a great deal of knowledge about their own community and its wildlife, resources, and unique characteristics. Governments can facilitate the organization of this type of information for use in formal decision-making by including citizens in government decision-making. Another critical component of managing risk is reducing information asymmetry (Ostrom, Schroeder, and Wynne 1993). Information asymmetry is a lack of access to knowledge, especially for those with few economic resources. Citizens may not be able to obtain information about their own consumption and their related environmental impact without the assistance of governments. For instance, labeling of organic food products, safety warnings on pesticide bottles, and fuel consumption averages on automobile stickers assist citizens in making informed decisions about the consumption of resources. The funding of research and education allows the public increased access to scientific knowledge. Governments and nonprofit agencies also can collaborate on gathering and sharing information that allows multiple groups or systems to understand how their decisions affect one another, again reducing risk. The collaboration between nonprofit, for-profit, and public organizations can motivate citizen action and education, create positive, tangible impacts on communities, elicit increased resources or increased efficiency in the use of resources, and allow multisystem and multilevel integration of sustainable development.

also MDT Ads in reducing asymmetry

Public administrators have to think about the impact of their decisions not only on the agencies within which they are employed, but also on a variety of related systems. Systems theories are a common approach to modeling environmental sustainability. They call for stakeholders to view communities from a wide perspective that considers not only each system of goods and services individually, but how they are connected and related to one another. Systems theories, like any theory, are an abstraction. Many things can be modeled this way: river basins, recycling flows, and financial transactions. Such models are characterized by box and arrow diagrams with the following components: inputs that affect a given condition (the system), which produces outputs, which then feed back to the environment, possibly affecting future inputs (Dye 1992). Systems theories fit nicely with the notion of "weak sustainability" presented earlier, which looks at different types of capital and their interrelationship (Roseland et al. 2005).

Sustainable development manages scarce resources in a manner that nurtures communication, coordination, collaboration, planning, and

Exhibit 1.1 **Community Systems**

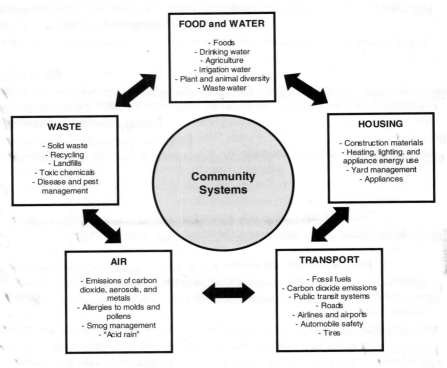

implementation between systems of service and goods providers. Sustainable development, using a systems theory approach, can be implemented in numerous types of organizations, including those that involve the following:

- construction or remodeling of buildings
- provision of public transportation systems
- development of alternative energy sources
- planning of public and assisted-living housing
- provision of K–12 and higher education programs
- management of wildlife
- agricultural management
- air quality regulation
- community and economic planning
- management of water for drinking and irrigation

A simple diagram of community systems suggests that food, water, housing, transportation, waste management, and air quality systems must be considered for human viability (Exhibit 1.1). This diagram does not include a variety of other meaningful systems, such as those incorporating wildlife, recreation, and employment. In the planning for sustainable housing communities, for instance, it is important to include agencies providing health care, education, and food. While the use of energy-efficient construction and appliances and renewable resources for building, heating, cooling, and lighting may be considered in the housing community development, the impact of the agencies' sustainability plan may be diminished if it fails to provide access to sustainable transportation to health care, school, or work. For good air quality, proper waste management and recycling, and access to clean water, the community must also rely on other agencies. Sustainable development requires collaboration not only because of increased efficiency due to reduced overhead or transaction costs, but because failing to do so may actually eliminate the net environmental gains of careful, devoted, but uncoordinated agency sustainability planning.

It is important to note that systems theories are not static, objective entities, but one of many theoretical abstractions that allow social scientists to translate, organize, describe, and communicate organizational and human behavior. Systems theories are descriptive models that may not characterize any real-world situation completely. The difference between a model and the real-world case is the difference between an architect's drawing and the actual building as constructed. The drawing translates the architect's vision to contractors and builders in a sort of shorthand. Systems theories describe a model of relationships between components. Practitioners must be aware that the application of sustainable development to real-world components is much more complex and much less static than the model. Ongoing dialogue between stakeholders improves the communication of changes as they occur within system relationships. For instance, technological development may change system opportunities, the role of stakeholders, and related action. An example is the shift in the role of farmers as growers of food. Technology has added the production of renewable, biofuel energy resources as a potential role for agriculture in recent decades. The role of any one group or component is flexible and faces the possibility of change. Essentially, the system, as a whole, is a moving target, and public administrators must be prepared for and adjust to changes, overlaps, and unexpected circumstances as they occur. On the other hand, the flexibility of real-world roles and components allows public administrators and community stakeholders to consider innovations in action planning and to continuously mold the action to the specific needs and assets of the community.

Do for MDT

Exhibit 1.2 **Examples of Inputs, Outputs, and Outcomes for Organizations**

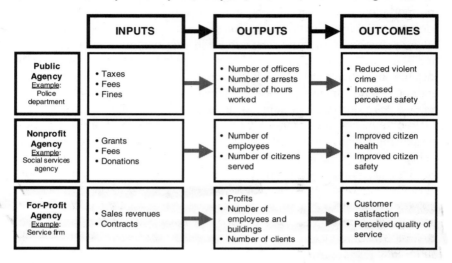

Measuring and Planning for Outcomes

Measurement and outcomes planning are also vital pieces of sustainable development planning. It is often difficult to know if agency actions have had a meaningful impact in meeting organizational and community goals. Because outcomes in service delivery are difficult to measure, it is hard to determine the return on investments of labor, capital, and time. Because resources are scarce and decisions must be made as to what services will be provided and who will be served, it is important to determine a link between inputs, outputs, and outcomes (Exhibit 1.2).

Inputs are investments in the resolution of identified problems. Outputs are the products created through that investment. Outcomes are the results of the action that the agency has taken to resolve problems of its choice. For instance, a recycling project may measure its outputs in terms of the number of tons of recyclables it processes in a year or the results of citizen use surveys, and define its outcome as citizen buy-in to recycling programs. A wildlife conservation organization may measure output in terms of the average number of animals of a particular species living in the wild and its outcome as long-term preservation of the species. The outcomes, because they hard to measure, are often stated in terms of single outputs. Even when outcomes are chosen as measurement, proxies are often used; in effect, organizations may use several outcome measures as a substitute for measuring goals in terms of outcomes. Defining goals in terms of outcome proxies improves the chances of understanding the impacts of planning, but can be problematic as well. This is because using several forms of measurement is resource-intensive and because individuals may fail to differentiate between outcomes and outcome proxies in their decision-making.

Developing good measures of inputs, outputs, and outcomes then enables managers to develop ratios that can serve as efficiency or performance measures. These ratios allow managers to compare one government to another or to make comparisons over time for a single government. For example, dividing the number of recyclables collected (an output) by the number of staff (an input) gives the amount of collections per worker (Martin and Kettner 1996). Dividing pollution reduction (an outcome) by the cost of these efforts (an input) gives us the cost per unit of pollution reduction. These measurements allow the government to chart its progress over time and to compare itself to another community or set of communities. This is valuable information for policy-makers and managers.

The measurement of outcome goals is especially important in a world of resource competition and diminishing abundance of natural capital. Nonprofit and government agencies are continuously invested in securing funding and resources. By demonstrating resource efficiency, organizations increase their competitive advantage for attracting and for maximizing the resources available to themselves and their constituents. Sustainable development can be applied at the input and output stages of human service delivery to increase outcomes or efficiency. Defining the outcomes then ensures that the right problems are being solved and that policies are effective.

Environmental Movements and Environmental Epochs in Public Administration

The U.S. Environmental Protection Agency (EPA) was established in 1970 as citizens advocated for better management of natural land, water, and air resources. Up to that time, many of the environmental issues were managed by the Department of Agriculture and the Department of the Interior. The work of the EPA, it was hoped, would establish research-based national guidelines for environmental decision-making and improved coordination and oversight of environmental resources. Several important environmental laws were passed to address environmental health. Among the most important are the Clean Air Act (1970), the Comprehensive Environmental Response, Compensation, and Liability Act (1980), the Federal Insecticide, Fungicide, and Rodenticide Act (1996), the Federal Water Pollution Control Act (1977), the Resource Conservation and Recovery Act (1976), the Safe Drinking Water Act or Clean Water Act (1977), the Endangered Species Act (1973), and the Toxic Substances Control Act (1976). Each of these laws represents a segment in the evolution of environmental policy and decision-making in the United States. Although the 1970s were a great era of progress for environmental preservation in the United States, regulation alone was unable to produce the full extent of desired results.

The 1970s mark a period of increased government and nonprofit investment in the management and protection of the natural environment. In looking at sustainability within the context of public administration, it is important to tie the history of public administration to the epochs of the environmental movement. According to Mazmanian and Kraft (2001), there have been three epochs of the environmental movement: the regulation for environmental protection period, the efficiency-based regulatory period, and the sustainable development period.

The first of the three epochs, from about 1970 to 1990, was concerned with the development of legal administrative and regulatory infrastructure. By ensuring compliance with federal and state regulations, this infrastructure prevents businesses from introducing negative externalities into the environment and the economy. Citizens are compensated and protected by government when their property rights to the use of the environment are violated. Efficiency-based regulatory reform, focusing on economics, was the trend from the 1980s to 1990s. Internalization of externalities, testing for cost-effectiveness, reliance on the private marketplace, and greater stakeholder and public participation were signatures of this era. The era from 1990 to the present is described as the "era of sustainable communities." This era

---

An Act to Remember
The Clean Air Act (1970)

The Clean Air Act is one of the most important federal environmental laws in the history of the United States of America. The act regulates air emissions from both stationary (e.g., factories) and mobile (e.g., automobiles) resources. It also establishes the National Ambient Air Quality Standards, which are designed to protect the environment and public health. This act continues to play an important role in managing carbon dioxide emissions, acid rain, ground-level ozone, stratospheric ozone depletion, and air toxics. A review of the act informs the current policy focus on reducing global climate change as a result of carbon emissions in the United States and internationally.

S. Dev.

reemphasizes environmental preservation, requires the use of planning and assessment tools with a focus on multiple, overlapping systems, and considers both human and natural resource needs (Mazmanian and Kraft 2001).

Sustainable development becomes the tool for matching legal and economic incentives. By combining regulation and economics, public and nonprofit organizations encourage citizens and private business to adopt behaviors and practices with great environmental benefits. By considering macrolevel and microlevel issues, long-run and short-run outcomes, and multisystem impacts, governments and organizations can ensure that environmental sustainability is approachable as a practice as well as a philosophy.

Tenets efic
effectiveness
responsiveness
equity

Sustainable Development as a Renaming or as New

The tenets of public administration, such as efficiency, effectiveness, responsiveness, and equity, find new life through the application of environmental sustainability and sustainable development. A number of relevant terms have received both political and policy attention in the last few years. They are introduced here and will be discussed further in later chapters of this book. The greenhouse effect and climate change, ozone depletion, atmospheric acidification, toxic pollution, biological species extinction, deforestation, land degradation, desertification, depletion of nonrenewable resources, and urban air pollution and solid wastes are all symptoms of "unsustainable development." Public administrators, placed in the role of managing efficiency and resource availability in the short-run, are increasingly addressing these issues through sustainable planning within their agencies. California, New York, Massachusetts, and Minnesota are leading the way in sustainable development, and a number of other states are integrating sustainability into statewide agency programs. Sustainability may be an emerging tenet that assists public administrators in reducing the risk of crisis-level resource depletion in their communities.

Public administration is comfortable with the adoption of proverbs or principles that are then used to educate practitioners and theorists as part of the normative orientation of public administration (Simon 1946). The appeal of sustainability and of sustainable development to the language of public administration is not in the creation of new concepts, but in considering concepts already important to public administration simultaneously. Sustainability offers academics and practitioners a new vision of public administration in which key principles are not opposites competing in dichotomous relationships, but rather complementary values. Sustainable development packages the tenets of public administration differently, allowing organizations and citizens to plan for future generations. This book will tie these tenets to the more exacting considerations of sustainable development.

15

Questions to Consider

1. Do you believe sustainability is a foundational philosophy of public administration? Should it be placed with tenets such as efficiency, effectiveness, and responsiveness in public administration education?
2. What do you see as the primary environmental issues facing your community? How are public and nonprofit organizations addressing these issues?
3. Focusing policy and advocacy on the environment is not a new trend in public administration practice in United States. What are the similarities and differences between past environmental initiatives and the recent focus on sustainable development?

area of focus or capstone?

2

Economics and the Environment

Sustainability is about resource use, and economics is the study of the allocation of scarce resources among competing alternatives. While many disciplines are relevant to sustainability, economics is at the core of any discussion of this topic. There are many misconceptions about economics. Some environmentalists see it as inherently focused on profit and money. While these are topics within economics, the focus of economics really is on efficient use of resources. Efficiency here takes on a very specific meaning. Efficiency can be defined as a situation in which there are no more gains to trade available (Nicholson and Snyder 2007, 365). Gains to trade are available where two or more parties could trade and both would come away from the trade better off or equally well off. When all these potential gains are exhausted, the economy can be considered efficient. Thus, an efficient economy uses resources to their highest value.

There is no reason to believe that an efficient economy will be fair, or equitable. Social equity can be defined in many ways: to each an equal share, to each according to merit, to each according to need, and so on (Winfrey 1998, 20). Some people believe that inequalities of all kinds should be reduced or eliminated, while others see inequalities as the natural result of differences among people in their talent, effort, or endowments. In any case, the process of reaching an efficient allocation and the resulting distribution of wealth and income may or may not fit with any one view of equity.

Most economists see the appropriate resolution of this conflict between efficiency and social equity as an effort to strike a balance between the two values (Okun 1975). Both social equity and efficiency are valued social goals, and ideally citizens would want to achieve both. Of course, this balance may not be possible, as some choices present a trade-off between the two goals. For example, taxes on labor income are likely to affect (either increase or decrease) work effort thus reducing efficiency. However, tax revenue is needed to run government programs. Thus, many economists advocate raising tax dollars as efficiently as possible—by minimizing the efficiency loss per tax dollar raised. Inevitably, as taxes go up, inefficiency increases, presenting this equity-versus-efficiency trade-off to decision-makers.

When applied to the environment, the framework of an efficiency trade-off is very compelling. Everyone would like to have clean water and air, but how much are citizens willing to pay for them? While citizens do not pay for clean air directly the way they pay directly for a bag of groceries, they do pay for environmental quality indirectly through taxes, the prices of regulated goods, and restrictions on actions that pollute. Scientifically it is easy to make water pristine, but it can be done only at great cost. Reducing greenhouse gases can be achieved by reducing or eliminating the use of the internal combustion engine, but how many people are willing to give up the use of cars and accept much higher costs for goods now delivered by trucks, trains, planes, and ships—or forgo the use of these goods? The economic insight is that trade-offs such as these are the essence of decision. It is easy to choose a cleaner environment if there is no social cost to doing so, but it is not so easy when people have to give up money or freedom of action in order to gain environmental quality.

This chapter will introduce economic concepts and apply them to the environment and the goal of sustainability. While there are limitations to the potential of economic approaches to address the problems raised by the world's unsustainable path of development, we see such approaches as central to the framing and resolution of these issues. Further, to be fair to the science of economics, we present the mainstream viewpoints of economics.

Markets and Market Failure

A market can be a physical market or, more commonly, a network of producers and suppliers linked together through production and distribution systems. Economists often speak of "the market for oil" or any other commodity. To be a little more precise, there is no single market for a commodity, but many. This multitude of trading connections means that more than one price may often be charged for identical or similar goods. That said, it is easier to talk about a single market with a single price. While this wording may not be descriptively accurate, it is not far off in most cases.

Markets, or, more accurately, the process of trading, allow producers and consumers to exchange goods for mutual benefit. Achieving gains through trade is one of the great insights of economics. If two people voluntarily trade and both are better off as a result, this is a gain in economic efficiency. Further, most economists would say that society is better off as a result of this trade. Generally, this is true; in fact, this is how value is created. If an entrepreneur can make a profit by hiring labor and buying other inputs to production and transforming them into an output worth more than the cost of the inputs, the resources of society have been harnessed in a productive way. The resulting output is greater in value than the inputs, and at least one person is better off, and no one is worse off.

Markets provide incentives and signals that structure people's economic decisions. When a good is in high demand and low supply, the price will rise, signaling to producers that they can make more profit by producing more of the good. As they do so, the supply of the good will increase, and the price will drop. More people will be able to get the good, and both buyers and sellers will be better off. In a similar way, prices provide signals to consumers. When the price of a good increases, consumers need to think carefully about whether they should continue to purchase the good. Some will continue to do so if the value of the good to them is greater than the price. This difference between value and price is known as consumer surplus; it is a measure of the economic value received by consumers. Other consumers will stop buying the good because the price is greater than the value to them; that is, their consumer surplus if they were to buy the good would be negative. This is an efficient response. It is efficient because those who get a positive consumer surplus will get the good, and those who do not, will not. This response may or may not be fair.

Markets generally do a good job of producing and distributing goods when there are no major equity issues and when the market functions well. The impediments to market efficiency are of four general types:

- The good is a public good, such as public safety, which is consumed jointly.
- The consumption or production of the good involves external costs or benefits to others not involved in the transaction.
- There is a lack of competition in the production and/or consumption of the good.
- There is an imbalance of information between the buyer and seller.

The following discussion focuses on the first two issues.

CHAPTER 2

Public Goods

Public goods stand in contrast to private goods. A public good is one which several people can jointly consume together with little or no effect on each other, whereas for a private good, consumption is rival rather than joint. For example, either you get an apple or I do; we cannot both consume it at the same time, so an apple is a private good. But public safety is a public good because it is consumed jointly. If a community is safe from crime and fire, all citizens benefit; one person's enjoyment of this safety does not diminish that of another person. This feature is known as nonrival consumption. Another related concept is nonexcludability, which means that it is difficult or impossible to exclude people from the consumption of the good once it is provided.

Private goods are rival and excludable. Public goods, such as public safety, national defense, and clean air and water, are both nonrival and nonexcludable. Two other types of goods can be delineated here:

- Toll goods, which are nonrival and excludable (such as cable TV or Internet access)
- Common pool goods, which are rival and nonexcludable (such as drilling for oil or fishing in the ocean)

These distinctions among goods are important because they identify which types of goods must be provided by the government and which do not. Public goods need at least some degree of government involvement in their provision because there needs to be a collective decision on the level of the good provided. Because all citizens consume public goods jointly, they all need to articulate their preferred level of the good for the provision to be economically efficient. Although most people provide some level of fire safety for their property, it would be prohibitively expensive for each person to provide the level of fire safety most citizens have come to expect. So they rely on the public provision of fire safety services. All citizens are affected by the government's decision about what level of fire safety services to provide (and consequently about how much citizens have to pay in taxes for this service). While government need not directly provide all public goods, there does need to be collective decision-making in the provision of these goods.

This collective decision-making is not necessary with private goods. You can choose to spend a lot of money on nice clothes and live in a modest apartment, while I may make the opposite decision, and neither of us is affected by the other's decision. Toll goods and common pool goods are more complicated. Toll goods can be provided privately, as cable TV is, because it is feasible to

The Tragedy of the Commons

In 1968, in his presidential address to the Pacific Division of the American Association for the Advancement of Science, biologist Garret Hardin warned of the "tragedy of the commons." He described a pasture open to all the cattle of different herdsmen. The herdsmen have an incentive to graze their cattle as much as possible, as grazing increases the value of their stock, and they do not have to pay for it. However, once the commons has reached its capacity, overgrazing will deplete the resource until it eventually becomes barren. The tragedy is that each herdsman acts in rational self-interest, leading to collective disaster. In Hardin's words, "each man is locked into a system that compels him to increase his herd without limit—in a world that is limited. Ruin is the destination toward which all men rush. . . . Freedom in a commons brings ruin to all" (1968, 1244).

charge people to subscribe for the service. However, some people will thus be excluded from use of the service. These goods are nonrival in consumption, so there is little additional cost to extend service to other consumers, and many would value the service. Consumer surplus could be increased at little cost. Of course, if this service were provided free to all, the question of how to pay for it would remain, as there would be no revenue from the subscribers. Public provision is possible, but so is private provision. Some mixture of the two is usually chosen for these types of goods.

Common pool goods are particularly interesting for the issue of sustainability. As described, they are rival but nonexcludable. Fish in the ocean are a good example. In a big enough body of water it is practically impossible to stop people from fishing. Obviously the fish are worth something in the market, so people have an incentive to catch as many as they can. But then the stock of fish can become depleted and eventually exhausted. This situation is often referred to as the "tragedy of the commons," after the famous article by Garret Hardin (1968) described above.

We see the tragedy of the commons in many situations. Overhunting, depletion of minerals and fresh water, and congestion are all examples of this problem. There are a variety of ways to address these problems. One simple approach is to establish ownership. If the commons were owned, then the owner would have the incentive to protect it: for example, by limiting grazing to a sustainable level. Note that this is a market solution that harnesses the profit motive for the betterment of society. However, it also limits access to those willing and able to pay. There are other solutions. The commons could remain as a public resource, but its use regulated by rationing it. Or other creative ways could be developed: taking turns grazing on alternate days, asking for volunteers to maintain it, or taxing the community to maintain it. Hardin described the use of property rights to solve this problem as unjust, but acceptable in some situations because "injustice is preferable to total ruin" (1968, 1247).

What is the right thing to do? The answer depends on several factors, such as legal institutions, the degree of social integration, community wealth, the ability to enforce laws, technology, and what people will accept as politically fair. As would be expected, different societies have resolved these types of problems in different ways. One of the underlying principles of economics is that the structure of society creates incentives that then shape the solutions that are possible. Appropriate incentives are therefore critical to long-term social and economic development. A healthy society offers incentives that lead people to add to the wealth of society, rather than detract from it. In fact, this was one of Adam Smith's points in his classic book, *The Wealth of Nations*, first published in 1776 (1909). Therefore, an unsustainable system is not only bad for the environment, but also bad for the economy.

Externalities

As mentioned above, externalities are external costs or benefits of a transaction that affects others besides the two making the exchange. For example, you decide to plant a flower garden in your yard that I can see from my yard. You work hard to maintain the garden and pay all the expense. I enjoy the benefit of your consumption decision at no cost. This is a positive externality in consumption—positive because it is a benefit, and related to consumption because it is a consumption decision you make. A negative externality in consumption would be any decision you make that creates a cost or negative effect for me, such as playing music I do not like, smoking, driving a polluting car, or using hazardous chemicals in your yard that leak into mine. Externalities in production can be positive or negative too. The classic negative production externality is air or water pollution from manufacturing. An example of a positive externality is research by one company or university that can be used by another.

As these examples illustrate, externalities are common occurrences in daily life. Some are minor and can be resolved easily. If your music is too loud, I can ask you to turn it down. If I enjoy your flowers, I can thank you by baking you cookies or helping you rake your leaves or shovel snow from your walk. A healthy fabric of society and a healthy set of economic institutions reinforce the resolution of many of these externalities. In other cases, they will not be resolved privately. A power plant polluting a river that flows through many states or provinces creates a complex problem that affects thousands, perhaps millions of people. The owners of the power plant will probably not want to make any changes in its production that increase its costs, and the people affected may be too disparate and unorganized to negotiate directly with the factory. Further, political and economic power may hinder the resolution of the problem. If the factory owners are politically and economically stronger than those harmed by the pollution, then the pollution may well continue.

Resolution of serious externality problems is important, not just for environmental quality or fairness, but also for economic efficiency. When markets fail, potential gains from trade are not realized. If the water pollution were reduced, those gaining would in theory be able to compensate the losers and both would be better off. Missing this opportunity means that society is not using its resources as well as possible. However, it also has another important implication: that *some* level of pollution is usually better than a zero level. Despite the problems it creates, pollution is the by-product of valued productive activities, such as traveling in cars, food processing, steel manufacturing, and so on. Unless technology makes a zero-pollution process possible, people have to accept some pollution in order to enjoy these productive activities. Therefore, the goal is to balance the negative externality of water pollution against the production of electricity that is essential in modern life.

The economic rule in this situation is to *internalize* the externality; that is, to take the external cost into account in the decision-making of the producer and the consumer of the good. The separation of the external cost from the transaction was the cause of the problem in the first place, so the solution should correct this error. Similarly, with a positive externality, people enjoying the production or consumption decision of another should do something to show the value of the good to them. Maybe I should buy the flower seeds and fertilizer for the flower garden you planted. This will reduce the cost of the garden to you and encourage you to plant more flowers, which we both will enjoy.

Addressing Externalities

Externalities can be internalized in a variety of ways. One approach is to tax a negative externality and subsidize a positive externality. For example, the government taxes the purchase of tobacco and alcohol because the consumption of these goods hurts not only consumers but others as well. The government subsidizes research and immunization because many people benefit from these goods in addition to the producer and consumer. This approach is known as a Pigouvian approach, named after the French economist A.C. Pigou (1946), who first suggested it. This approach can work well because it creates a financial incentive that affects both parties to the externality-causing transaction. If the level of the tax or subsidy is right, it will cause both parties to adjust their consumption to the efficient level. In the case of a negative externality, both are likely to bear some of the burden of the tax, and the government will also generate funds that it can use to address the problem. The difficulty here is getting the level of the tax or subsidy right, as doing so depends on having clear information on the financial value of the externality.

A second approach is to subsidize the reduction of a negative externality. This approach is commonly taken by the U.S. government, which pays subsidies to state and local governments and firms to research and implement pollution-reduction technologies. However, this approach creates two problems. An equity problem arises in using public tax dollars to subsidize polluters to reduce their emissions, especially when bigger polluters get bigger subsidies. Second, a distributional problem is created by this subsidy as it increases the profits of polluting firms, thus attracting new firms to the industry and possibly causing more pollution (Cropper and Oates 1992, 681).

A third approach is regulation. For example, the government selects the economically efficient level of pollution and then allows the producers to emit this level. This policy raises a number of questions. When will the pollution be permitted? Will the regulation apply to the company as a whole, to each of the company's factories, or to each of the factory's smokestacks? Should all companies be allowed to emit the same amount of pollution, or should the level depend on factors such as the amount of their output, their location, and their ability to pay? What should be done when other environmental conditions (wind, heat, pollution from other locations, and so on) affect air quality? As these questions suggest, while regulation seems sensible at first, the details are potentially very complex. In the case of air and water pollution, regulation has been found less efficient than other approaches, such as emissions trading (described below) (Winston 2006, 50–52). In other, less complex cases, regulation makes sense. For instance, many cities restrict where people can smoke cigarettes or drink alcoholic beverages, when people can run a lawnmower or enter public buildings, and which residents are allowed to see certain types of movies. These are somewhat simplistic approaches, but if they are commonly understood and accepted, they can work.

A fourth approach is to assign property rights to one of the parties involved. This is an ingenious approach that recognizes that the problem of externalities is a type of common pool goods problem. Because no one owns the air, people pollute it without legal sanction. If someone *did* own the air, the owner could sue polluters under a well-functioning legal liability system. The polluters

24

The Chicago Climate Exchange

The Chicago Climate Exchange, established in 2003, provides a market for its 350 private, public, and nonprofit member organizations to exchange emission allowances for greenhouse gases. The members commit to reducing their aggregate emissions by 6 percent by 2010. Legally binding, independent, third-party verification is done by the Financial Industry Regulatory Authority. Members trade carbon financial instrument (CFI) contracts much as stock exchanges trade stocks and bonds. "For instance, National Farmers Union's Carbon Credit Program is a multi-state program that allows farmers and landowners to earn income by storing carbon in their soil through no-till crop production and long term grass seeding practices. Farmers Union has earned approval from the Chicago Climate Exchange to aggregate carbon credits. Farmers Union is enrolling producer areas of carbon into blocks of credits that will be traded on the Exchange, much like other agricultural commodities are traded" (*Wikipedia* 2008; Chicago Climate Exchange 2008).

---

could then offer to pay for the right to pollute in amounts and at times that could be specified in a contract. Ronald Coase (1960), who won the Nobel Prize in Economics in 1991, asserted that under certain conditions, the establishment of property rights and the functioning of the market would lead to an efficient outcome. This method also has the advantage of compensating those harmed by the externality, which the tax and regulatory solutions do not do. However, there are some practical limitations to this solution. The first difficulty, of course, is deciding who owns the property right, as it affects the balance of power and the distribution of income. Legal liability is not fully articulated in all cases, many people do not have easy access to the legal system, and there are limits to the damages that can be collected because firms may declare bankruptcy or delay payment by appealing the ruling. While the practicality of this approach may be in question, it is an alternative for governments to consider in attempting to achieve an efficient outcome.

The idea of clearly defined ownership has led to the development of emissions trading policies. Emissions trading has recently been applied in the United States to address the problem of acid rain and in the European Union to reduce greenhouse gases. Recently, in the implementation of the international Kyoto Protocol, cap and trade provisions have been applied for six major greenhouse gases. This approach works by capping the amount of pollution allowed and issuing (or selling) allowances, which are permits specifying the allowable level of pollution for each permit-holder.

Permit-holders then can trade permits. If one polluter can reduce its pollution below the level allowed by its permit, it can sell some of its allowances to a heavier polluter who needs them. Over time, this process creates an incentive for polluters to reduce their emissions, as they will be able to make money by selling unneeded allowances. The polluters who can most efficiently reduce their pollution will do so, at a lower total cost to society, and the financial transfer from the heavy polluter to the light polluter may well be an improvement in equity.

Economic theory has suggested a number of ways to address problems of externalities. Moving from the abstract role of theory to the real world of policy implementation, the specific details of a given situation become the key factor determining the best approach. As Cropper and Oates write, these details include "the determination of fee schedules, issues of spatial and temporal variation in fees or allowable emissions under permits, the life of permits and their treatment for tax purposes, rules governing the transfer of pollution rights, procedures for the monitoring and enforcement of emissions limitations, and so on. In short, economists must be ready to 'get their hands dirty'" (1992, 731).

Cost-Benefit Analysis

How should people make decisions about the level of government intervention? More specifically, once citizens decide that a public good should be provided, what is the appropriate level of provision? Similarly, once they decide to reduce pollution, how much reduction is appropriate? Most economists believe that cost-benefit analysis (CBA) is the appropriate tool for making this decision. The basic principle of CBA is simple: add up all the benefits and costs of a proposal and calculate the net benefit by subtracting the costs from the benefits; accept the proposal if net benefits are positive, and do not accept it if net benefits are negative. There are more complex details associated with CBA, but they do not need to be discussed at this time. Done properly, CBA will lead to increasing social welfare, since only projects that increase social wealth—and, indeed, all such projects—will be selected. In many ways, CBA is the social equivalent of a profit/loss analysis of a private company.

Although CBA is a useful tool, its application in federal government projects is limited to certain situations. Executive Order 12291 requires CBA for all regulations having annual costs in excess of $100 million. CBA is also required for setting standards in the Toxic Substances Control Act and the Federal Insecticide, Fungicide, and Rodenticide Act. However, in other legislation, such as the amendments to the Clean Air Act of 1970 and the amendments to the Clean Water Act of 1972, it is explicitly *not* allowed

26

(Cropper and Oates 1992, 675–676, 723). Thus, the application of CBA is uneven, and the efficiency of federal environmental policy is mixed. This is the result of conflicts over the goals of policy. While increasing social wealth is one goal, other goals, such as social equity and environmental quality, may be in conflict with each other, leading to conflicting approaches for determining the level of government intervention.

A number of elements of CBA have had important influences on environmental policy. An elaborate set of procedures has been created in order to appropriately value environmental assets. This task is challenging, because many assets are never traded. For example, what is the value of the Grand Canyon? Despite these challenges, economists have made significant progress in identifying the value of natural resources, allowing citizens to compare the value of preservation of these assets to other measures of economic progress, such as increases in income.

The Economics of Sustainable Development

So far, this chapter has presented economic concepts that are central to understanding markets and the shortcomings of markets as applied to environmental issues. The next step is to demonstrate the place of economics in sustainability. Economics is central to sustainability because the normative goal of economics is efficiency—the use of society's resources to provide the greatest satisfaction. Any form of waste—pollution, undersupplied public goods, or distortionary taxes or subsidies—is inefficient. Sustainability requires not merely the reduction of waste, but also the elimination of processes that either have undesirable by-products or do not use resources effectively. Efficiency is a part of sustainability. More specifically, efficiency is a necessary, though not sufficient condition for sustainability. Efficiency is a necessary condition because in the presence of unrealized gains to trade, resources are not being used to their fullest. However, it is not a sufficient condition because there are many other dimensions of sustainability.

Sustainable policy has been defined as the provision of the same level of goods and services with nondeclining values of total capital (Pearce, Markandya, and Barbier 1989). Total capital includes natural capital (environmental assets), human capital (the stock of human knowledge and abilities), physical capital (buildings, machinery, equipment), and financial capital (stocks, bonds, and other financial assets). To achieve sustainability, all assets must be used in a way that increases, or at least does not decrease, the value of total capital. Many economic decisions transform one form of wealth into another. According to this definition, such transformations are sustainable if the net change in wealth is positive. For example, it is sustainable to harvest a forest

27

if the wood can be sold and the funds used to create a financial asset of greater value or invested in education that creates human capital of greater value. Thus a sustainable economic policy will increase social wealth. In this way, sustainability and economic growth are consistent. Also, policies to reduce market failures may enhance sustainability as well.

The United Nations Economic and Social Commission for Asia and the Pacific (2001, 3–10) has identified four dimensions of sustainability:

- Environmental: The use of natural capital should be limited to levels that can be replaced by natural regeneration.
- Economic: Goods and services provided must be cost-effective and achieve the highest social return on physical and natural capital.
- Financial: The activity should attract sufficient funds to cover capital and operating costs in the long term.
- Social: The consumption of natural capital must be balanced with improvements in the standard of living and the quality of life, particularly to reduce poverty.

Notice in this approach the similarity of the fourth dimension (social sustainability) with social equity. This approach suggests that the balance of efficiency with social equity can be supplemented with two other goals: environmental sustainability and financial balance. While there is no single framework that all sustainability advocates will or should agree upon, this approach is a very helpful one that identifies the main objectives of sustainability. As described here, the economic dimension supports the other dimensions of sustainability, and they in turn support it. The key here is that the return on capital assets should be the highest possible *social* return, not just the return to private investors. For example, if there is a negative externality, then the social return will be less than the private return.

Economic values are not the only ones that apply to sustainability, but they are central. Together with environmental conservation, social equity, and financial balance, they provide a framework for considering policies and the trade-offs that inevitably arise when citizens, organizations, and governments face challenging issues. A perfect system would achieve all these goals, but when this is not possible, there needs to be a structured way to evaluate the choices.

The next chapters apply these objectives to a wide variety of policy areas. Ultimately you will need to decide for yourself which choices are right and how citizens should collectively make decisions for the future.

Questions to Consider

1. Identify a situation characterized by the tragedy of the commons. What steps are being taken to address the problem? Do they work? If not, what might work?
2. How well does emissions trading work? Search the Internet for updated information on this innovation.
3. If a program had negative net benefits but helped the needy, would you favor it? If another program had positive net benefits but benefited only the rich, would you favor it? If you answered "it depends," what does it depend on?

Good question for discussion

3

Managing Risk as the Work of Governments

In late August 2005, the Atlantic saw the formation of a hurricane that was to have an immense impact on the politics, economics, and social welfare of U.S. citizens. Gaining power as it crossed the Gulf of Mexico, Hurricane Katrina caused the deaths of more than 1,800 people, the abandonment of 200,000 homes, and the loss of 190,000 jobs in New Orleans (ABC News 2006). Ten months after the storm, only 70 percent of oil production in the gulf was restored to pre-Katrina levels, a significant reduction for the United States, which obtains 29 percent of its oil from the region (ABC News 2006).

Delays and failures in emergency response left many New Orleans citizens stranded following levee breaches and massive flooding. The disaster influenced and continues to influence decision-making and planning by a number of public and nonprofit organizations. The National Response Plan first focused on local control of emergency situations. Coordination between local, state, and federal actors became increasingly complex as the crisis escalated. Government agencies faced a great deal of criticism from citizens as the crisis unfolded and after the storm subsided, when relief was slow in coming. Federal-level agencies such as the Federal Emergency Response Agency (FEMA) and the Coast Guard had to coordinate decision-making with local police forces and fire departments, as well as with state-level responders. Nonprofit organizations also were impacted by the 2005 hurricane season. For instance, the American Red Cross raised $2.11 billion in designated donations to the victims of the 2005 hurricanes, forcing the agency to adjust its donation and services policies very quickly under increased citizen and donor scrutiny (American Red Cross 2006).

In addition to problems with the response to the emergency itself, a great deal of concern has been aimed at the engineering of the levees in greater New Orleans and on the development of land below sea level and prone to flooding. Decisions on the original development and on redevelopment also encountered a great deal of multilevel government politics. Local zoning and planning decisions and recommendations by the Army Corps of Engineers continue to contradict each other on a number of important issues. Today, concerns remain about the risks of reinvesting in the region. The costs of redevelopment with the near certainty of future flooding in parts of New Orleans, for instance, may be too high for the citizens of the nation, as a whole, to support. Citizens must rely on the technical knowledge provided by experts to determine the costs and benefits of rebuilding the region.

Finally, the crisis also forced additional attention on the issue of global climate change as the scientific community and political advocates suggested links between hurricane storm intensity and ocean warming patterns. The magnitude of the problem shifted from hurricanes' impact on local and state communities to potential impacts internationally. The complexity of the problem increased to include discussion of the reduction of carbon dioxide emissions in order to reduce the advance of global climate change. The problem was now viewed as an environmental one. Governments and nonprofit organizations had to engage with risk at a macrolevel, seeking larger scale solutions. These solutions can work only in collaboration and coordination with international communities and their stakeholders and require action plans that involve multiple levels of government simultaneously.

As discussed in Chapter 1, one of the roles of government and nonprofit organizations is to reduce risks to citizens and to introduce and foster stability in uncertain circumstances. In the management of complex problems, governments and nonprofit organizations provide coordination of services, education, information, expert assistance, and oversight. They also facilitate communication between multiple agency actors and numerous stakeholders. As the boundary of the community is extended, the number of stakeholders becomes increasingly difficult to identify and engage (Exhibit 3.1). Stakeholders interact and have overlapping roles and responsibilities within systems of citizens, civil society organizations, and local, state, federal, and international levels of organizations. Individual citizens, due to limitations of resources of money, time, and knowledge, and perhaps due to some level of disinterest, may be unable to tackle such problems without assistance from the public sector. This suggests that governments and civil society provide a mediating force in the management of crises, including those involving environmental issues such as global climate change, fossil fuel depletion, air pollution,

Exhibit 3.1 **Systems of Stakeholders**

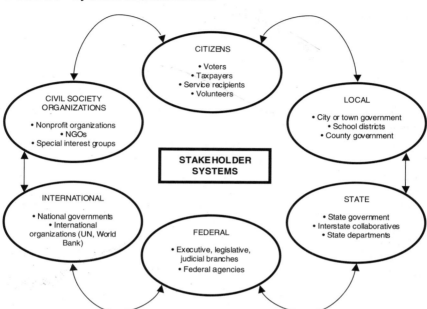

waste management, water scarcity, food quality and scarcity, and reduction in biodiversity. Sustainable development is an attempt by public administrators to manage human behavior and natural systems with the goals of improving social and economic welfare. Also, through the use of incentives and regulations, public administrators can increase equity in distribution of limited and scarce resources (Leuenberger and Wakin 2007).

The problems related to Hurricane Katrina came forward in layers. Often, as in the case of this tragedy, a number of embedded problems surface together in a time of crisis. These interrelated problems intensify risks before a crisis and magnify the impact of the tragedy at onset. During and after Hurricane Katrina, problems such as economic inequity, engineering failures, increased environmental uncertainty, political dysfunction, gaps in communication, and coordination failures contributed to the threat to citizens' well being. When multiple systems interact in a community, public administrators have increased difficulty in assessing the hazard level. When environmental degradation occurs, discovery of the extent of the peril may occur only when the environment has reached its carrying capacity. Although a community may face very small, incremental levels of degradation, a point may be reached at which remedy is not possible. Public administrators must identify subtle changes before they aggregate to crisis levels. Sustainability planning is a tool to manage these subtle changes so that short-run decisions are less likely to lead to long-run catastrophes.

Time and Place Knowledge and the Value of Citizen Engagement

In 2001, the Environmental Protection Agency (EPA) initiated a citizen engagement program titled Small Communities Outreach Project for Environmental Issues, known as SCOPE. The mission of the program was to engage water-testing professionals and well owners in decision-making regarding the introduction of additional chemical treatments to drinking water in selected communities (Leuenberger and Wakin 2007). Wells with multiple users, such as hotels, campgrounds, and schools in rural areas, were to face additional regulation. After gathering extensive scientific evidence on well-water treatment in the American Midwest and on well-water chemical treatment in general, the EPA solicited advice from the well owners on the rule-making process. The program also increased citizens' participation by providing education on the rule-making process to stakeholders and by sending facilitators from academic institutions to engage citizens in rural sites. The citizens offered valuable advice on the water quality of individual wells, the impact of geological characteristics, and user demographics. They also explained that the quality of water in some wells, specifically those situated in sandy soils, was actually better with no chemical treatment. The citizens' concerns about the costs of chemical treatment and the disposal of chemical by-products also were discussed.

Sustainable development planning integrates experiential time and space information held exclusively by citizens (Leuenberger and Wakin 2007). Governmental organizations coordinate the participation of stakeholders, gather technical and scientific knowledge, and arrange for mediators or facilitating agencies as appropriate (Exhibit 3.2). This information gathered from technical and citizen experts ensures that short-run and long-run plans are rooted in a deep understanding of the relevant science and technology, associated human behaviors, and the natural environment itself (Leuenberger and Wakin 2007; Leuenberger 2006). The tension between professional and citizen knowledge leads to improved decision-making. Collaborative arrangements emerge out of the understanding that neither citizens nor administrators can consider themselves the sole proprietors of the public interest (Simonsen and Robbins 2000).

Sustainable development also requires an understanding of the role of civil society as a catalyst and facilitator of citizen engagement with govern-

Exhibit 3.2 **Citizen and Government Engagement**

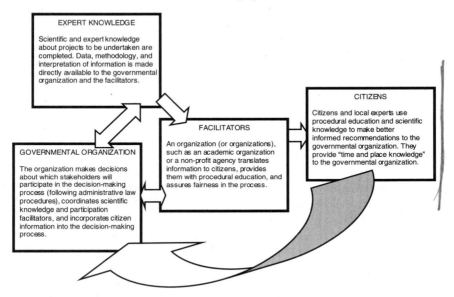

ment (Leuenberger and Wakin 2007). Civil society can be defined as an integrated, structured relationship of community, voluntary organizations, government, and business, wherein rights and responsibilities are placed in balance (O'Connell 1999; Leuenberger and Wakin 2007). The participation of citizens is especially crucial as these stakeholders interpret and modify rules of the community based on their own beliefs and desires (Gibson, McKean, and Ostrom 2000). A strong civil society recognizes the existence of a problem, renegotiates social contracts between stakeholders, develops individual responsibility, and uses multiple systems and levels of government to solve problems (O'Connell 1999; Leuenberger and Wakin 2007). Citizens and nonprofit organizations address gaps in services or risk management not covered by governments (Ostrom 1990).

Inter- and Intragenerational Equity and Planning for the Long Run

Public administrators working with sustainable development are interested in two types of equity. First, they consider equity among groups of citizens in the existing community. Scarce resources, especially those associated with fundamental human needs such as food, water, and shelter, are redistributed by governments in order to meet established social and ethical standards. Second, public administrators consider the impact of short-run decisions on the long-run welfare of future groups of citizens. Thus, as time horizons shift, both intergenerational equity and intragenerational equity are addressed. Public administrators seek not only to establish equity between groups of citizens alive today, but also to manage today's resources so that future generations will also enjoy a standard of living at current levels or better.

One type of sustainable development, broad-based sustainable development, moves beyond long-term environmental preservation and resource management to include a focus on citizen participation and equality. Broad-based sustainable development requires a healthy, equitable, growing economy centered on reaching a high standard of human welfare, preserving human rights, advancing civil society, and investing in democratic participation (Weaver, Rock, and Kusterer 1997). Public administrators, using this perspective, must also consider the distribution of resources at the international level and the equity of resource distribution in countries with varying levels of economic, technological, and political development.

Process, Administrative Law, and the Rights of Citizens

Although inclusion of citizens in decision-making is a key component of planning in public administration, it is important to note that the level and type of participation are not always easy to establish. Citizens may engage with governments in a number of ways, both receiving information from and providing information to decision-makers. A citizen may play the role of voter, taxpayer, and consumer or service recipient, participating in all, none, or any combination of these roles. In addition, citizens interact with a number of levels of government simultaneously and may also have differing levels of engagement based on the bundle of goods and services they receive.

Further, the type and extent of involvement may be at least partially determined by established administrative law, procedure, and practice. Public agencies in the United States follow the guidelines of the Administrative Procedures Act, which outlines the rule-making process and attempts to standardize and define rule-making. When certain agency rules are proposed, the agencies must provide opportunities for formal public comment. For instance, in the case of well-water treatment discussed above, stakeholders had the right to review the rule as published in a government document called the *Federal Register*, to provide oral or written comment, and to review the final rule thirty days before it took effect. Rule-making requires that any newly adopted rule must follow legislative intent and may not be a stricter procedure than that imposed by the legislature. While allowing stakeholder communication on agency decision-making outside of the voting process, this citizen participation process requires the careful adherence to a formal set of standards.

In addition to being involved in agency decisions through rule-making, citizens may be invited to participate in strategic planning, including planning on sustainable development issues. This form of participation, established by the agency within the guidelines of the Administrative Procedural Act and parameters of legislation, may include direct involvement of citizens on the decision-making committees, written survey responses, oral survey responses, a review of data involving exit interviews at the close of specific services, representation of citizens through special interest groups and advocates, and focus groups. In addition, information provided by citizens to direct-line workers may also be used in decision-making. Direct-line workers have face-to-face contact with the individuals they serve and therefore have the opportunity to collect information about citizen preferences and needs. In environmental sustainability planning, it is critical that citizens' voices are heard in order to ensure that citizens will be politically and behaviorally aligned with the plan of action.

Does the Environment Have Rights?

The rights of citizens are critical in sustainability decision-making, but does the environment itself have rights? In a classic work titled *Should Trees Have Standing? Toward Legal Rights for Natural Objects*, Christopher D. Stone discusses the possibility of rights and representation for the natural environment. Originally published in 1972, it points out that most of the legal history of the United States measures the extent of environmental damage only in terms of damage to the property of human beings. Because rights are a social construct, structured by human beings based on their social, political, religious, and cultural ideologies, it is possible, he suggests, that human beings could grant rights to nonhuman environmental players. Further, certain public and nonprofit agencies may act as advocates or guardians of natural objects, including wildlife, trees, rivers, air, land, and oceans.

In thinking about sustainable development planning, the rights of humans and of natural environment stakeholders are critical. Although legal rights are available only to current citizens, public agencies often provide protection to nonhuman species as well as to future generations of citizens through the decision-making process. The protection of the environment often overrides short-run concerns about property and extends to long-run benefits to societies and to nature. For example, state and federal governments regulate human interaction with endangered wildlife species by placing restrictions on particular properties. This can infringe upon private access for those planning to use these properties for hunting, fishing, waste management, and development. These infringements upon the actions of individual citizens are seen as an adequate price to pay for the long-term survival of species in communities in which such regulations are promulgated. Public administrators again must negotiate between levels of government and jurisdictions in order to ensure the congruence and fairness of such decision-making for all human and nonhuman stakeholders.

Government and Its Partners

Governments have the ability to transform their communities through sustainable development. The inclusion of citizens and stakeholders in decision-making, incorporation of time and place knowledge and technical expertise, protection of citizen rights, and planning for inter- and intragenerational equity are opportunities for governments to make a difference in environmental sustainability. The government is a collaborator in and a facilitator of civil society action. The partnership of governments with stakeholders is a critical part of its responsibilities. Because of these opportunities and responsibilities, public administration can make a strong contribution to environmental sustainability.

Questions to Consider

1. Create a diagram of stakeholders affected by Hurricane Katrina in 2005. What responsibilities do governments have in the coordination of multiple stakeholders in crisis situations?
2. What is the role of government and civil society in preventive planning?
3. How involved should citizens be in public agency decision-making?
4. Should rights or guardianships be established for natural objects in the environment?

4

Nonprofit, For-Profit, and Public Agents

Many organizations have implemented plans for environmental sustainability or are considering doing so. All organizations have the opportunity to reassess their service and production infrastructure in order to institute more sustainable practices. In addition to the implementation of sustainability within the organization, it is important to understand the various roles and responsibilities made possible to external stakeholders as well. With increasing competition among private organizations and with limited money, human, and natural resources, the individual and joint action of agencies is critical. Which organizations should lead educational, research, advocacy, policy-making, regulation, fundraising, and action tasks to promote sustainability and what are the roles of actors within various sectors? This chapter will answer these questions.

Both private and public agencies have a role to play in environmental sustainability. The systematic relationship of community, voluntary organizations, government, and business, wherein rights and responsibilities are placed in balance, constitutes civil society (O'Connell 1999). Civil society has the potential to foster changes leading to sustainability. Public organizations create and implement policies, provide intervention and educational programs, and manage market failures by regulating private organizations, directly managing common pool resources, and providing funding for research and programs. Private nonprofit organizations act as advocates for specific segments of the environmental system, providing political and educational support for citizens and their leaders. They also offer a number of important services and products not provided by private for-profit and public organizations, filling gaps in the community's environmental, economic, and social well-being. Private for-profit organizations, motivated by consumer demand, are also a valuable partner in environmental sustainability. Especially in recent years, green consumerism is expanding the revenues of private for-profit organizations as well as providing additional economic resources for environmentally conscious production.

Privatization, as governments contract and collaborate with private organizations, has begun to blur the roles of private and public agency stakeholders in sustainable development planning. Although the responsibilities of public and private organizations are increasingly elusive (Savas 2000), the legal, financial, and strategic structures of private for-profit, private nonprofit, and public agencies differ at a number of levels. The structure, mission, and leadership of organizations have a strong impact on their roles in community decision-making and development. Exhibit 4.1 outlines the traditional leadership structures, guiding principles, fund-raising mechanisms, and political influences on private and public organizations. Important responsibilities within sustainability-focused action include citizen education and inclusion, policy development and implementation, efficient production and provision of goods and services, technology and research development, and management of market failures. How organizations choose to include tenets of sustainability in their planning, how they define their roles, and how organizations interact with each other in addressing environmental issues are critical to meaningful sustainable development in communities. Private and public organizations, with or without primary mission focus on environmental issues, can be contributors to sustainable development.

Nonprofit, for-profit, and public organizations have increasingly included sustainable development in their agency planning process. Using tools such as strategic planning, mission restructuring, and environmental commitment statements, organizations are considering environmental sustainability and resource efficiency in construction, production, and provision. Early attempts to include environmental sustainability resulted in plans that were external and separate from the organizations' strategic planning process. More recently, organizations are integrating sustainability into multiple levels within the larger agency plan and tying it directly to resource efficiency management. Integration has been a vital advance in sustainable development planning. As organizations manage their own resources more efficiently and reduce their consumption of nonrenewable assets, they build long-term viability for themselves and their communities.

Nonprofit Charitable, Volunteer, and Environmental Organizations

Nonprofit and nongovernmental organizations have contributed significantly to sustainable development across the world. For the purposes of this discussion, the term *nonprofit* refers to corporations identified as holding 501(c)3 status in the United States. These organizations provide a wide range of services and products, including environmental protection and education, human welfare assistance, development assistance, and citizen education. Nongovernmental organizations include not only nonprofit organizations, but also organizations with similar purpose and status outside the legal structure of the United States. Charitable organizations operating in a number of international settings are identified as nongovernmental organizations (NGOs). NGOs, which register and operate within the guidelines dictated by the nations in which they complete their work, are important partners with governments on economic, social, and infrastructural development. These organizations provide advocacy, build and warehouse knowledge, educate citizens, guide collaboration, and promote research.

A number of nonprofit and nongovernmental organizations promote sustainable development by providing protection to environmental entities that do not have legal rights. The Sierra Club, for instance, has been advocating on behalf of the environment since 1892. The World Wildlife Foundation has offered protection to fragile environments and endangered animals for over forty-five years. Because nonprofit organizations have the ability to specialize, they may gain very specific information about environmental issues. The missions of such organizations clarify the specific goals and tasks that the agencies are willing to undertake in order to promote sustainable development (see Exhibit 4.2). For instance, the National Audubon Society has not only focused on environmental well-being as a component of its work, but is a specialist in wildlife management. It has unique knowledge of bird species and provides sanctuaries and education centers for preservation of natural resources. Its members serve as advocates, research partners, fundraisers, donors, and educators. By building with and on community assets, the Audubon Society combines a number of program goals under its mission "to conserve and restore natural ecosystems."

Education and service are a part of environmental action driven by nonprofits. For example, Roots and Shoots of the Jane Goodall Institute engages youth by acting as an umbrella for environment- and peace-related service projects. Classrooms, clubs, and neighborhood groups that register with the organization receive the tools and guidance they need to pursue community projects tied to the environment and to peace.

Nonprofit organizations provide expertise and resources that are important to planning, decision-making, and action. However, there is a great deal of overlap in service delivery by nonprofit and nongovernmental organizations with a primary environmental focus and therefore a growing need for collaboration. A number of coalitions allow agencies with shared goals to share information and resources as well.

Exhibit 4.1

Roles of Private and Public Organizations

	Private nonprofit and nongovernmental organizations	Private for-profit organizations	Public organizations
Guiding principles	Mission-driven decision-making	Mission traditionally driven by profit and consumer demand	Mission-driven with influence from political leadership and government policy
Selection of service or product recipients	Recipients determined by mission, designed by leadership	Provision determined by ability to pay	Recipients determined by mission, influenced by government policy
Leadership	Traditionally led by a board of directors and an agency director	Traditionally led by a board of directors and a chief executive officer (CEO)	Traditionally led by appointed top management and career midlevel management
			Appointed leaders changed with shifts in elected officials
Influence of politics	Increasing privatization and government contracts blurring the line between government and private organizations	Advocacy tasks kept within legally specified limits	Government regulation of private for-profits to manage market failures is an important component of environmental and economic policy making
			Policy and practice decisions of government organizations heavily influenced by political leadership
Fund-raising	Donor giving	Consumer spending	Taxation
	Government contracts	Stockholder funding	Fee for service
	Fee for service	Government contracts	Borrowing

Sustainability roles			
	Education of citizens	Efficient management of provision and production resources	Development and implementation of sustainability-related practices and policies
	Advocacy for and protection of wilderness, wildlife, and environmental capital	Adherence to regulations and policies related to sustainable practices	Protection of natural capital
	Efficient management of provision and production resources	Research, development, use, and promotion of sustainability technologies	Brokering of information related to sustainability
	Research, development, use, and promotion of sustainability technologies		Education of citizens
			Inclusion of citizens
			Funding of research and development
			Management of market failures and common pool resources

Exhibit 4.2

Sample Mission Statements of Nonprofit Organizations With a Primarily Environmental Focus

National Audubon Society: To conserve and restore natural ecosystems, focusing on birds, other wildlife, and their habitats for the benefit of humanity and the earth's biological diversity. (National Audubon Society 2008)

Roots and Shoots of the Jane Goodall Institute: To foster respect and compassion for all living things, to promote understanding of all cultures and beliefs and to inspire each individual to take action to make the world a better place for people, animals and the environment. (Roots and Shoots 2008)

Woods Hole Research Center: To understand the causes and consequences of environmental change as a basis for policy solutions for a better world. (Woods Hole Research Center 2008)

National Resources Defense Council: To safeguard the Earth: its people, its plants and animals, and the natural systems on which all life depends. (National Resources Defense Council 2008)

World Wildlife Fund: The conservation of nature. Using the best available scientific knowledge and advancing that knowledge where we can, we work to preserve the diversity and abundance of life on Earth and the health of ecological systems by protecting natural areas and wild populations of plants and animals, including endangered species; promoting sustainable approaches to the use of renewable natural resources; and promoting more efficient use of resources and energy and the maximum reduction of pollution. (World Wildlife Fund 2008)

Nonprofit organizations also partner with for-profit organizations to meet their mission-guided goals. For instance, the World Wildlife Fund partners with private donors and with for-profit organizations such as Nike, Wal-Mart, IBM, Hewlett Packard, Toyota, Nissan, Johnson and Johnson, and the Coca Cola Company to drive action to preserve endangered species. The maintenance of healthy environmental systems and management of economically viable organizations are not mutually exclusive. In fact, with greater consumer focus on environmental issues, partnerships between for-profit and nonprofit private organizations may be mutually beneficial.

Planning, collaboration, and mission focus are important for strong environmental sustainability. Action, however, also is a necessary component of meaningful sustainable development work. The National Resources Defense Council, for instance, leads action on a number of environmental issues and also provides citizens with knowledge about policies and about personal lifestyle changes. Private nonprofit and nongovernmental organizations with a primary environmental focus typically have in common an action-driven mission, collaboration with citizens and private organizations, and educational programming. These organizations then provide to agencies whose focus is not primarily related to environmental issues the opportunity to learn from, borrow, and implement production and service processes to decrease their negative environmental impact.

Research and technological development are also important contributions of nonprofit and nongovernmental organizations. The Woods Hole Research Center and the International Institute for Sustainable Development, for example, both focus on research on sustainable development as part of their mission goals. Organizations such as these offer researchers the opportunity to share knowledge with citizens and to serve as centers for collection and dissemination of data. Action driven by research and careful data analysis is more likely to result in successful achievement of community environmental goals.

Finally, a number of organizations support human welfare by supporting healthy environmental systems. Organizations provide research, education, and action on issues such as renewable energy, safe food and water, transportation, recycling, waste management, global climate change, air quality, and construction. Because the time and money costs of gathering information on sustainable lifestyles are high, these organizations increase the community's social, natural, and economic capital by making knowledge accessible to citizens.

The Potential of For-Profit Contributions to Sustainability

The role of private, for-profit organizations in contributing to environmental sustainability is largely underplayed in public administration literature. According to Donna Kennedy-Glans and Bob Schulz in *Corporate Integrity* (2005), for-profit businesses have the ethical responsibility to exceed compliance standards and to engage in action with integrity and accountability. The authors suggest that ethical and decision-making tools can be used to manage responsibilities that include natural capital preservation and sustainability.

A number of private, for-profit organizations, large and small, have committed to environmental sustainability as a component of their planning process (Exhibit 4.3). In addition to serving as a marketing tool and meeting customer demand, sometimes for businesses with poor environmental sustainability records, environmental commitment statements often exceed government regulations and standards, focusing instead on practices that contribute to the long-term health of communities, the environment, customers, and the businesses themselves. By exceeding government policies and standards, organizations integrate some of the negative externalities of doing business into the cost of production and provision and contribute to the development of technologies that may lead to both greater resource efficiency and ecological welfare in the long run.

Ethically responsible actions by for-profit agencies can also transform entire production and distribution processes. Processes that use native, renewable resources, that recycle by-products of production, that eliminate the use of toxic chemicals and substances, that reduce waste in manufacturing and packaging, that employ energy-efficient building structures, and that reduce transportation from the production site to the consumption site are moving toward environmental sustainability. When the amount of time a product has to be stored is reduced, so are the costs of energy and construction for storage units. When native species are planted, the costs of water and of pesticides are reduced. When by-products are recycled, the costs of material and the cost of waste removal are reduced. In many ways, changing production systems to be more environmentally friendly may lead to cost savings in the long run, although initial investments in restructuring may be high. By having a long-run plan for change, organizations can consider the costs and benefits of several alternatives. Making changes when replacing equipment or undertaking small projects is a starting place.

In addition to small-scale changes, it is also possible to undertake structural changes that are larger in magnitude. Hawken, Lovins, and Lovins in their book *Natural Capitalism* (1999) suggest a large-scale change from production systems that turn out disposable goods to a system whose products are built to be renovated and reused. Instead of buying a new automobile every few years, for instance, consumers would have a car built in such a manner that technological innovations could be adapted to it as they occur. Instead of exchanging a computer, car, washing machine, or television for new ones, the consumer would have the unit renovated periodically. This would, of course, reduce costs of production and reduce waste. Unfortunately, the current system of consumption and economic growth is not tied to reusable goods. The infrastructure of entire systems would need to be reassessed and redesigned in order to accommodate this new method of production. The irony of creating new and innovative systems for reusable goods is that they are not so new. Until the 1940s, for example, glass milk bottles were commonly filled by the local dairy, delivered to the consumer's door, and then collected and reused in the United States. This method continues to be used by some dairies in the United Kingdom.

In creating new systems of production, partnerships between governments

Exhibit 4.3

Sample Environmental Commitment Statements of For-Profit Organizations Without a Primary Environmental Mission

Wal-Mart: Environmental focus on energy and resource conservation, use of renewable resources, and reduction in the use of raw materials used in their store operation and construction. (Wal-Mart Stores 2008)

Hewlett-Packard: HP is committed to providing customers with inventive, high quality products and services that are environmentally sound and to conduct our operations in an environmentally responsible manner. That commitment continues to be one of our guiding principles that are deeply ingrained in our values. It is from this history and these values that HP has become a leader in delivery of environmentally sustainable solutions for the common good. HP meets this commitment with a comprehensive environmental, health and safety policy, strict environmental management of our operations and worldwide environmental programs and services. (Hewlett-Packard 2008)

The Walt Disney Company: is committed to balancing environmental stewardship with its corporate goals and operations throughout the world. (Walt Disney 2008)

The Coca-Cola Company: is focused on the areas where we have the most significant and visible impacts—water stewardship, sustainable packaging, and energy and climate protection. (Coca-Cola 2008)

Toyota: We, Toyota Motor Corporation and our subsidiaries, take the initiative to contribute to harmonious and sustainable development of society and the earth based on our Guiding Principles. We comply with local national and international laws and regulations as well as the spirit thereof and we conduct our business operations with honesty and integrity. In order to contribute to sustainable development, we believe that management interacting with its stakeholders . . . is of considerable importance and we will endeavor to build and maintain sound relationships with our stakeholders through open and fair communication. The three sustainable concepts that contribute to society are pursuit of sustainable manufacturing, technological innovation, and social contribution activities for building a sustainable society. (Toyota 2008)

IBM: IBM is committed to environmental leadership in all of its business activities, from its operations to the design of its products and use of its technology. IBM's corporate policy on environmental affairs, first issued in 1971, is supported by the company's global environmental management system, which is the key element of the company's efforts to achieve results consistent with environmental leadership and ensures the company is vigilant in protecting the environment across all of its operations worldwide. (IBM 2008) and businesses are often necessary. Political and economic incentives offered by governments must match visions of environmental sustainability and maintain the integrity of individual private entities. The role of citizens is especially important as public and private agents act based on the economic and political voice of their constituents. Subsidies and policies that encourage renewable energy use and development, that credit the use of recycled and reused capital, and that are tied to local production systems will build more sustainable systems.

The Power of Public Agencies and the Costs of Sustainability

As discussed earlier in this chapter, the transaction costs of sustainable action are high, sometimes making it difficult for citizens and organizations to implement and practice sustainable development. A transaction cost is the price of doing business. It includes the costs of information-gathering, research development, and contract development and enforcement. Public agencies act as information and research funding brokers, reducing the costs of transactions to individuals.

Besides offering the policy and financial incentives for private organizations to undertake sustainability projects, governments also provide education, incentives, and information to make environmentally conscious lifestyles available to citizens. By controlling policies, regulations, and incentives, government agencies can promote sustainable development. In the United States, state governments have had a large role in implementing sustainable development. California, New York, Massachusetts, Minnesota, Washington, Oregon, and Arizona are examples of states that have implemented a number of policies on sustainable development. Some have mandated all their state agencies to also create internal sustainability plans. Local governments have also been groundbreakers in sustainable development; cities such as Seattle, San Francisco, Boston, New York, and Portland, Oregon, have implemented strong action plans for environmental sustainability.

In addition to state and local initiatives and policies, which are bottom-up processes, there are top-down processes as well. The nations of the European Union (EU) provide a strong example of the top-down process. Many of the planning and funding structures for local-level governments are highly centralized. For instance, the financial instrument supporting environmental and nature conservation projects throughout the EU, as well as in some candidate, acceding, and neighboring countries, is a program called LIFE. Since 1992, LIFE has co-financed some 2,750 projects, contributing approximately €1.35 billion to the protection of the environment in member countries of the European Union. Both the bottom-up and the top-down approach to environmental planning have unique strengths. The advantages of the top-down approach include ability to implement large-scale projects, a tendency toward funded rather than unfunded mandates, implementation of a minimum standard of conduct for private stakeholders, and centralized access to information on technological innovation and environmental data. The strengths of the bottom-up approach include greater buy-in and contribution at the local level, greater opportunity for citizen inclusion in decision-making, greater freedom for private stakeholders to manage their own sustainability outcomes, and increased ability to match action to the specific characteristics of each community. Examples of both types of approaches in development will be introduced in future chapters.

Government organizations, by supporting citizen education and information access, also encourage sustainable development. As discussed in earlier chapters, governments are already in the business of reducing risk to citizens. The labels attached to a can of soup, a package of cigarettes, or a used car window inform consumers about the product they are purchasing and ensure that the trade between seller and buyer is fair. This reduces the transaction costs of the exchange, leading to greater efficiency. Like these information mechanisms, data about the impact of products on long-run environmental and human health may one day be made available for citizen decision-making. This type of information allows citizens to be more responsible in how they use their economic voice to support sustainable consumption and production systems.

Planning Internal Agency Change

All organizations must be aware of their own assets, resources, talents, infrastructures, and missions in moving forward with sustainable development. Strong plans take advantage of the character and vision of the organization. The following tips may be helpful in guiding organizational planning:

- Leadership: Recruit, train, and empower champions at the upper levels of the organization and managers at all levels of the organization and include citizens and personnel in planning, training, and decision-making.
- Assessment: Complete an assessment of resources, mission, vision, and organizational goals before moving forward with planning. SWOT analysis, which explores internal strengths and weaknesses and external opportunities and threats, may be useful.
- Citizens: Ensure that citizens' economic and political voice is heard and that they have access to the data needed to make informed decisions.

CHAPTER 4

- Role: Consider the role and responsibilities of the organization within the community, including the nature of its private nonprofit, private for-profit, or public status.
- Plan: Explore existing plans and ensure that a current and comprehensive plan, such as a master plan or a strategic plan, are in use.
- Mission and statements of commitment: Integrate sustainability into the mission and/or draft a statement of environmental commitment.
- Resources: Consider tying sustainable development to each resource as it is expended in the production or service process and provide alternative actions within the formal planning document.
- Research: Carefully research alternative actions.
- Action: Ensure that action is the focus of all planning.
- Evaluation: Evaluate action and planning, making changes as appropriate.

Questions to Consider

1. What do you see as the role of private and public agencies in environmental sustainability planning?
2. How can private and public agencies contribute to citizen and organizational education related to sustainability?
3. What are specific challenges faced by organizations implementing environmental sustainability and how can these barriers be overcome?

5

Fresh Water

Water is probably the most valuable and the most undervalued natural resource on Earth. Most of the planet is covered in water, yet, according to the U.S. Geological Survey, only about 1 percent of water on Earth is fresh water. Most of that 1 percent is stored as groundwater and is critical for agriculture and for drinking water. Discussion of water is important to a discussion of sustainable development in public administration because of the importance of water to human welfare, its role in global and local well being, and its relationship to agriculture, international politics, and global climate change. Nonprofit organizations and governmental agencies are at the center of water resources management and decision-making worldwide.

The sustainability of fresh water impacts local, state, federal, and international stakeholders. It is a key component of community development, urban planning, and agriculture. The availability and quality of freshwater require management of individual consumption and the management of multiple, interconnected systems. Leadership of governments and nonprofit organizations is necessary to ensure fair distribution and property assignment, to regulate and manage negative externalities, to support research and build information, and to extend education to citizen stakeholders.

This chapter focuses on the availability and development of freshwater, the local to global nature of water, mechanisms for including citizens in water resource management, and the role of nonprofit and government agencies in protecting the availability and quality of freshwater.

Drinking Water and Development

According to a 2000 report by the World Water Council, an international body established by a collaboration of the World Bank, the United Nations

51

Development Program, and a number of other international organizations, increases in demand and limited supplies will lead to a significant "water gap" by 2025 (Conca 2006). Sixty percent of the world population lives in coastal communities with access to water, yet safe drinking water is already unavailable to 1.3 billion individuals worldwide and adequate sanitation is unavailable to 2.6 billion individuals (Ward 2002; Conca 2006).

The balance of water in the world creates interesting predicaments across the globe. Temperature, sea level, rainfall, the frequency and magnitude of storms, geographic characteristics, evaporation, river discharge, proximity to saline water, the availability of underground and surface freshwater, and water retention in the soil all affect the amount of freshwater available to citizens (Ward 2002). Population distribution, the types of production and economic development, and consumption behaviors of individuals also have a strong impact. A number of cases across the world highlight the dilemma.

Las Vegas, Nevada

The Las Vegas metropolitan area supports about 2 million residents and millions of visitors each year. The economy of the city is built on tourism, gaming, and convention accommodation, all of which require a large number of service workers. Huge pools and fountains in front of brightly lit luxury hotels would suggest an abundance of water, yet daily consumption for basic needs of residents and visitors is taxing the water resources of the region. Las Vegas is in a desert and, according to the Las Vegas Valley Water District, 12 percent of its water comes from underground sources. A large portion of freshwater also comes from Lake Mead, the water level of which is considerably diminished. In the summer of 2008 the surface was twenty to thirty feet below its average level; the lake is reported to be about "half full." The city of Las Vegas and surrounding communities have an extensive drought plan and conservation practices in place to manage water availability. With the growing demands from increased population and related increases in consumption, the long-term availability of fresh water in the Las Vegas area is at serious risk.

Dubai, United Arab Emirates

On the Arabian Peninsula, an emirate of high-rises is ever growing. Dubai, an ancient coastal trade center, has seen an astounding amount of growth and development in the last forty years. Dubai is building its economy on tourism and business, a bold move to divert the potential negative impacts on the economy of fossil fuel resources. It uses desalination for most of its freshwater needs, removing salts and minerals from ocean water by a series of energy-intensive processes. There are also potential long-term environmental impacts related to disposal of waste from the desalination process. The question remains whether Dubai will be able to sustain its current level of development and consumption in the long run.

Sihanoukville, Cambodia

Sihanoukville is a coastal city with about 235,000 residents and supports 300,000 tourists annually. The beaches and islands in the region offer game fishing and deep-sea diving. Soka Beach Sihanouk Ville, Cambodia's first five-star hotel, opened in 2004, and four other luxury hotels will be completed by the Sokimex Group by 2011. At the same time, the city has a large low-income population. Since 1991, the World Bank has supported water supply and waste management systems rehabilitation through the Sihanoukville Water Supply Authority (World Bank 2008a). By 2003, 18,000 people had received access to water supply services through this project. Rehabilitation of the ancient distribution system and capacity building through staff training continues, adding to the number of city residents with access to clean water.

Cartagena, Colombia

Cartagena is a key tourist destination in Colombia. The World Bank loaned $85 million (U.S. currency) to the city in 1999 in order to improve sewage, wastewater, and water supply infrastructure. By 2005, 99 percent of citizens had access to the water supply, up from 30 percent in 1994, and 95 percent of citizens had access to sewage systems. The investment was largely in poor neighborhoods, with 80 percent of the new connections in poor neighborhoods. More than 1 million individuals received services (World Bank 2008b).

The four examples above demonstrate the struggle of communities to meet their economic and environmental needs through development and growth. In the cities described above, several common threads emerge. All four cities are dependent on tourism for economic growth, have large disparities in economic well-being among residents, and are focused on freshwater as a key developmental issue. Each has a number of government and nongovernmental organizations working to create more sustainable access to clean, reliably available freshwater. Several goals can facilitate this sustainability. Sustainable development of water requires the following conditions:

- There is a match between available natural freshwater resources and human needs for drinking and agriculture.

- There is a cost-effective means for processing and distributing water to users.
- There is equitable distribution of water for basic human needs.
- There is adequate waste and wastewater removal from households and businesses to ensure the long-term quality of water.
- There is environmentally conscious disposal of water treatment by-products.
- There is continued access for natural systems that depend on the same water for their well-being.
- The structures and built environments accommodate natural systems and wildlife processes tied to the water systems.
- There is adequate balance between use and the recharge of water systems.
- There are effective legal, social, and economic incentives in place to manage consumption and pollution.
- There are effective education and research to support positive changes in consumer behavior, technological innovation, and environmental impact for long-run benefits.

The scarcity of freshwater is likely to continue to be the focus of development in the future. Global climate change, which may alter amounts of precipitation and temperature levels across the world, also may have an impact on communities. Some communities may be faced with more severe droughts, while other communities may have their freshwater supplies contaminated by flooding and the introduction of seawater into systems. Because a number of highly populated areas are already facing problems with freshwater access and wastewater removal, the problem could be intensified. The link between fresh water and agriculture also is adding to the dilemma.

Water, Irrigation, and Agriculture

In 1900, there were 600 big dams across the world. By 2000, there were 45,000 big dams in the world, with 300 of them considered major dams (Khagram 2004). In 1933, President Franklin D. Roosevelt signed the Tennessee Valley Act, authorizing river-basin control to develop a region covering parts of seven U.S. states (Ward 2002). The goals of dam and water control construction include flood prevention and hydroelectric energy production; however, another major outcome is agricultural development. The scarcity of water continues to be the single largest threat to food security across the world; approximately 90 percent of all national water budgets are tied to agriculture, and agriculture consumes the largest portion of freshwater used in the world (Postel 1999; Allan 2002; Ward 2002). Water for irrigation and land reclamation for farming are critical products of such development. With 17 percent of the world's crops being irrigated, the availability of freshwater through such mechanisms has a significant impact on the world's food supply (Postel 1999). For certain countries, the importance is even higher, with 100 percent of England's, 52 percent of China's, and 80 percent of Pakistan's cropland being irrigated (Postel 1999).

In the United States of America, the cases of two very different water aquifers, the Ogallala and the Plymouth-Carver, highlight the relationship between freshwater and agriculture.

The Ogallala Aquifer

The Ogallala aquifer is a shallow, largely underground, geological formation of freshwater underlying large parts of Nebraska, Kansas, and Texas and smaller portions of Wyoming, Oklahoma, South Dakota, Colorado, and New Mexico. The area produces large amounts of corn, soybeans, and wheat and is also an important ranching area. Forty percent of all beef processing plants and feedlots in the United States use the aquifer for freshwater resources (Glennon 2002). Most of the residents of the area obtain their drinking water from the aquifer as well. Unfortunately, the water levels in the aquifer are dropping. The water table dropped more than 150 feet in parts of Texas and Kansas between 1940 and 1999 (Glennon 2002). In addition, there have been reports of increases in pesticides and nitrates entering the water system.

The Plymouth-Carver Aquifer

The Plymouth-Carver water system is a sole-source aquifer, meaning it is designated by the Environmental Protection Agency as the only source of drinking water for most of the residents in the Massachusetts cities of Plymouth, Carver, and Wareham and in parts of Bourne, Kingston, and Plympton. Cranberry farming uses a large portion of the water consumed from this source. There has been increasing emphasis on reducing consumption and pollution of the water source by resident and agricultural users.

Both these cases illustrate the importance of water systems on food security in the long run. Agricultural producers are critical stakeholders in maintaining or improving water quality and quantity and have a huge interest in preserving water resources. Supporting collaborative plans that include these stakeholders is an important part of sustainable development for public administrators.

For most citizens in the United States, obtaining safe drinking water requires only the turning of a tap. Although the bottled water industry has boomed in recent years, the quality of water from taps is largely equivalent to that of bottled water, and using tap water eliminates the extra environmental costs of producing and transporting bottled water. Similarly, for most citizens, obtaining food requires merely a short trip to a grocer. Perhaps because of the ease of obtaining these necessities, most citizens are not aware of the sources of the food and water they consume. They may also be unaware of the direct relationship between their consumption and the quality of food and water resources. For instance, the nitrates and pesticides introduced by lawn and garden maintenance of individual citizens adds to the amount of nitrates and pesticides introduced into water systems through agriculture. Unlike farmers, however, individual consumers are subject to much less government regulation about the quantity of pesticides and nitrates they introduce into a system. This could result in too many undesirable chemicals in drinking water as pesticides leach into underground water systems from private properties. In addition, garden grown foods can be compromised and rendered less safe for human consumption by chemical overuse. Governments must rely on individual citizens to properly apply products to their lawns and gardens. This problem is called nonpoint source pollution, meaning that there are number of polluters, all of which cannot be identified and regulated. In order to solve the problem, individual consumers must understand the link between their own practices and the systems that support their basic needs.

Public administrators have several opportunities to work with citizens and agricultural producers to promote the quality and quantity of clean water. Some of following suggestions may be helpful in preserving freshwater for individual and agricultural consumption:

- Provide citizens with information on the source of their drinking water and its basic characteristics; their own level of consumption, recommended consumption levels, and potential tools for reducing their consumption; pesticide and fertilizer use; proper disposal of waste products such as oil and paint; and septic tank maintenance.
- Provide citizens and agricultural producers with economic and social incentives to adopt environmentally friendly practices.
- Use citizen surveys, land use data, and other types of research information to assist with decision-making.
- Use grassroots initiatives and existing community-led groups to promote improvements.
- Create regional water conservation committees to advise governments and citizens on water quality and conservation issues.
- Provide educational information to communities using multiple sources, such as newspapers, attachments to bills, radio spots, elementary and high

school presentations, community meetings, mailed fliers and pamphlets, web pages, and television spots.

- Provide sustainable development education to agricultural producers through entities such as the U.S. Department of Agriculture, state university extension services, and state and county agricultural and environmental agencies.

Local to Global Action

Another important aspect of freshwater management is its local to global nature. Unfortunately, most citizens view water scarcity as a local problem instead of as an important part of international social, political, and economic systems (Rothfeder 2001; Conca 2006). There are several reasons why public administrators may benefit from viewing water as a global issue. First, water management and trade have become an enormous economic industry across the world, involving the profits from the water trade, related property rights, and equity in distribution. Second, the interconnected nature of water systems requires joint planning and development across a number of levels of government and between various governments at the same level. Third, water is becoming a commodity linked to war and peace around the world.

Freshwater, which was once considered a public good, is now largely viewed as a private good. People are familiar with water from a tap or in a bottle, and the rights of property once the water has been packaged and delivered are relatively clear. Water as a natural resource is more difficult to define under property rights. The rights of ownership become complicated because water is an always-moving asset. Some seasons or years are drier or wetter than others. Some sources of water have the ability to fully recharge, while others do not. The space that underground aquifers and streams occupy regularly changes with shifts in the water system. Global climate change has been identified as another source of change, increasing flooding in some areas and drought in others, raising temperatures in some and lowering them in others. Further, freshwater on one piece of land may be fed by sources outside of that land. The rights of property over water have resulted in disputes and struggles worldwide. All these factors affect the rivalry and excludability of water, causing variation in its status as a public, private, toll, or common pool good.

For instance, the construction by Turkey of the Ataturk Dam on the Euphrates River increased irrigation and drinking water for Turkey, but significantly reduced water to Iraq and Syria (Ward 2002; Shapland 1997). Israel's National Water Carrier on the Jordan River following the Six-Day War of 1967 created disputes with the Arab League (Ward 2002). This construction project was undertaken to transfer water to high population regions in Israel and created tension over water with Jordan and Syria. Such disputes have important consequences for the residents of the regions involved. Obtaining enough water for agriculture and drinking water in communities with limited water resources is an ongoing struggle. The social, economic, and political impact is felt globally even when disputes may seem to be isolated and local.

Water is an important natural resource to consider within public administration because it is a vital system component of human survival and environmental well-being. Local water systems are interconnected, creating a local to global concern for management of water. Increasingly, public and nonprofit agencies are collaborating on water management, improving the quality of water, fish and wildlife habitat preservation, water availability, and flood control (Sabatier et al. 2005). Where there is war, conflict, or disagreement over water resources, the social systems that resolve distribution and access questions may break down. Government or nonprofit intervention may have an even more critical role during these times. On the whole, the tragedy of the commons, the problem of overconsumption and pollution caused by a lack of property assignment for water, may best be addressed in collaborative systems. Another option is to assign property rights to water, but both private and government ownership of water has resulted in unequal access to water and ongoing disputes between local to global governments.

Questions to Consider

1. What are the most critical water issues facing your region?
2. Do you view the competition for water resources worldwide as critical to security and peace? Please state why or why not.
3. What type of government and nonprofit interventions have been the most effective in improving the quality of water in your region? On the national scale? On the international scale?

6

Food Security and Safety

Food security and safety are a critical component of sustainable development. Thousands of nonprofit and nongovernmental organizations focus on food security as part of their mission. Governments at all levels provide food redistribution assistance; oversight of labeling, distribution, and packaging; agricultural support; and education and information to citizens and organizations. Since food and drinking water provide the cornerstone of human health and well-being, the number of organizations offering related assistance is not surprising. Some examples of food security, safety, and production issues are:

- Undernourishment is a problem for 16 percent of the world's population (United Nations World Food Program 2008). International organizations struggle with economic, social, political, and environmental challenges in a quest to eliminate or at least reduce world hunger.
- In 2006 in the United States, 10.9 percent of households were food insecure sometime during the year, meaning that they did not have access to enough food for a healthy and active life (Nord, Andrews, and Carlson 2007). This example does not address the also serious impacts on health of eating unhealthy food and overconsuming. Redistribution of food products, education, and dissemination of information about healthy eating are among the tasks undertaken by governments and nonprofits.
- On an annual basis, the food-borne illness salmonella affects approximately 1.4 million people worldwide and had the economic cost of nearly $2.5 billion (USDA Economic Research Service 2008a). Because today foods travel thousands of miles from their point of origin, the role of governments in tracking food-borne illness is critical.

- In 2006, the National School Lunch Program operated in 101,000 schools, serving 28 million low-cost lunches per day and expending $8 billion (Ralston et al. 2008). The low-cost school lunch program in the United States is an example of collaboration between multiple levels of government, requiring coordination between school districts, states, and the national government.
- The United States exported 1.24 billion bushels of wheat products in the 2007–2008 market year, approximately 22 percent of all wheat exports worldwide (USDA Economic Research Service 2008b). The U.S. Department of Agriculture is a major collector and disseminator of data on agricultural food production in the United States and across the world.
- The rise in fuel prices in 2008 had a significant impact on food prices and therefore on global food security, especially in urban communities in high-risk areas (FEWSNET 2008). Organizations such as the Famine Early Warning Systems Network (FEWSNET) and the U.S. Agency for International Development (USAID) maintain data on weather, global climate change, economic indicators, political factors, and other variables that affect food production. These data are critical to an effective, on-time response to food insecurity.

Food security is closely linked to global climate change, political stability, economic stability, disease control, availability of freshwater, and transportation. As a component of sustainable development, food security is a strong indicator of human and environmental health. Many systems and systems components, at the micro- and macrolevels, must be in balance to maintain or achieve food security. Public administration makes a significant contribution to achieving this balance, through public and nonprofit agencies.

The Role of Public Administration in Food Safety and Security

Food security is a problem of distribution, rather than scarcity, on the global scale. Food is not equitably available due to political, social, environmental, and economic factors (Shiva 2000; Boucher 1999). Famine also is tied to war and violence for many at-risk populations (Swan and Vaitca 2007). Food insecurity is caused not only by natural systems variables, but also by failures of the free market (Lappe, Collins, and Rosset 1998). Public and nonprofit agencies can address food insecurity by filling in gaps in distribution, taking on market failures, and remedying information asymmetry.

Public and nonprofit organizations provide the following services and goods related to food security:

- Maintain and share distribution and scarcity data
- Maintain and share information on natural and climate-related variables tied to agriculture
- Maintain and share price and economic data
- Provide information and education on food safety, nutrition, and health
- Provide information and education on agricultural best practices, including the use of pesticides and fertilizers
- Define and standardize terminology and certifications in agriculture and food production generally
- Coordinate food security response data for emergency distribution decision-making
- Directly redistribute food resources to individuals at risk and in need
- Address barriers to food security caused by politics, violence, and war
- Regulate food safety labeling, packaging, and distribution
- Provide information on food safety risks and problems as they occur as a preventive measure
- Support scientific research on social, economic, biological, and political factors affecting food security
- Provide political and economic support to address policies and laws resulting in food security inequities globally

This list suggests that the role of public administration as it is tied to sustainable development and food security is largely coordination and sharing of information and knowledge. As stewards of the land, agricultural producers have strong incentives to manage natural resources in a manner that is environmentally sustainable into the long term. Some farmers engage in sustainable farming practices and work diligently to protect water, soil, and food quality and safety. Their work allows public and nonprofit agencies to partner with agriculture to ensure that development is as sustainable as possible. Public administrators can offer incentives for improved environmental health and provide educational and research tools to encourage meaningful action and real-world solutions for food insecurity. Making these incentives part of the framework of a sustainable system and enforcing them is the role of public administration.

Plant Diversity and the Green Revolution

One of the primary criticisms of food security intervention by public and nonprofit agencies has been the unbalanced support of scientific solutions for hunger prevention (Shiva 1992, 1999, 2000; Swan and Vaitca 2007; Lappe, Collins, and Rosset 1998; Boucher 1999). The scientific movement, termed

Coming to Terms
Sustainable Food Production Terms

The following terms are used frequently in describing the degree to which food production is considered sustainable:

Food security	Access to the quantity and quality of food necessary to keep people healthy and satisfied.
Food safety	A component of food security; assurance that food is free from chemicals and other substances that endanger health.
Organic agriculture	Agriculture that avoids the use of animal by-products and synthetic pesticides and fertilizers.
Antibiotic-free	Food products grown, manufactured, and stored without the use of antibiotics.
Nitrates	Nitrogen-containing compounds in water and food products that can pose a health hazard if consumed in large amounts.
Carrying capacity	The limit or boundary at which natural systems can maintain, recharge, and repair themselves under the strain of consumption, pollution, and use.
Biodiversity	Variation in all animal and plant species and subspecies.
Monoculture	The elimination of multiple species and adoption of a single species for food production.
Cage-free	Animals that are raised for food production without the use of cages (they may be confined by other methods).
Free-range	Animals that are raised in non-confined facilities for food production.
Sustainable agriculture	Farming that seeks to protect natural resources, use environmentally friendly practices, and supports the long-term welfare of consumers and producers.
Fair trade	A movement encouraging fair pricing for goods on the global market and elimination of poverty through environmental and socially responsible action.
Free trade	An economic model supporting free-market economies at the international level and very limited government intervention in trade.

the green revolution, focuses on solutions such as bioengineering to manage food production. Critics, however, object to the resulting reduction in biological diversity and the loss of local and indigenous species, since only a limited number of species are used in agriculture; the introduction of nonreproducing seeds that require repurchases from the same vendor for future years of planting; potential mixing of engineered and indigenous species; and the need for additional pesticides and fertilizers for growing species not well suited to certain growing regions.

Public and nonprofit organizations are stakeholders in the debate about the green revolution as funders of research and as advocates of political and policy views related to the issue. They also have a large role in defining property rights tied to bioengineering. As discussed in earlier chapters, property rights, when clearly defined and assigned, eliminate some of the problems associated with market failures. Property rights assigned to certain goods can generally ensure their protection and preservation. In the case of property rights to living entities, however, a number of inequities can occur. In general, property rights to living species are not legally supported in the United States. An individual can own a horse, but cannot have the right to ownership of all the members of the species that is defined as the biological entity "horse." Following this principle, the assignment of property rights to specific species of plants has been criticized for creating inequities tied to food security (Shiva 1995, 1999, 2000). Patenting certain species of bioengineered or naturally occurring species of plants, it has been argued, puts centuries of agricultural knowledge and development related to food species management at risk. For instance, a number of rice and soy species indigenous to India, species that took centuries to develop, may be altered slightly and then patented (Shiva 1995, 1999, 2000). The argument is against monoculture. Another equity issue is that making minor changes to what was considered a public good in a community and then asserting property rights to turn it into a private good eliminate access by the original users of the good.

Sustainable development requires using legal and institutional incentives and tools while carefully balancing scientific and technological advancement with attention to local and indigenous knowledge and practices. As populations across the world grow, especially in urban settings, the stress on agriculture to produce enough food is always increasing. The carrying capacity of food production systems requires careful consideration of the long-term impacts of the struggle to maintain or improve human welfare in the short run.

Systems Relationships and Food Production

Food production is tied to a number of other systems and systems components also impacting environmental sustainability. It is important to identify

Exhibit 6.1

Systems Components and Relationships With Food Production

Water	Fresh water is used extensively in agricultural irrigation. Chemicals, such as nitrates, from pesticides and fertilizers used in agriculture can enter water systems, posing a health risk.
	Nutrients from agricultural fertilizers can enter freshwater systems and affect biological systems; for instance, increasing the algae bloom and reducing available dissolved oxygen for fish species.
Transportation	Food often is transported great distances from its point of origin, taxing nonrenewable fossil fuel resources.
	Food prices rise with rises in oil prices, increasing the intensity and magnitude of food insecurity for some people.
	Food assistance programs must anticipate the time and costs of transportation in order to meet emergency needs during redistribution of food products.
Air quality and climate change	Transportation of food products increases the amount of carbon dioxide released into the environment, damaging air quality and contributing to global climate change.
	Food production is directly affected by temperature changes and related changes in rainfall.
Wildlife and oceans	Nutrients from agricultural fertilizers can enter fresh and saltwater systems, affecting wildlife survival, reproduction, and health.
	Land used for agriculture can infringe upon habitat.
	Bioengineered species can interbreed with naturally occurring species, impacting natural ecosystems.
	Monoculture in food production can result in losses to biodiversity.

and briefly discuss the relationship of food security to these other systems. Exhibit 6.1 describes the relationship between these components and food production.

Assistance with food security and safety is one of the major contributions that public and nonprofit agencies can make to sustainable development and sustainability. The work of organizations in the provision of abundant, safe, nourishing, and environmentally sustainable food to citizens exemplifies both the challenges and opportunities of sustainable development.

Questions to Consider

1. What do you see as the appropriate role of governments in managing food security? In managing food safety?
2. What are the primary threats to food security in your community?
3. Explore several nonprofit organizations that have food security as part of their mission and agency goals. What types of programs and services do they offer?
4. Identify international communities in which food security is currently at risk. List specific economic, social, political, and environmental factors impacting food security in the region.

7

Solid Waste Removal and Management

In 2006, 251 million tons of trash were discarded in the United States. Of this amount, approximately 32.5 percent was recycled (U.S. EPA 2008a). The United States, which has in residence about 4 percent of the world's population, is responsible for approximately 30 percent of the world's waste (Rogers 2005). Yet solid waste removal, for most citizens, is a privately or publicly handled service that is largely invisible. Most citizens do not focus on trash management unless there is a mishap, such as a trash strike, mishandling of hazardous materials, or failed pickup. Because tons of rubbish are removed from towns and cities each day swiftly, efficiently, and, in most cases, with little direct personal costs to citizens, solid waste management is rarely on the mind of citizens. It is, however, a very heated political and economic issue in many local government meetings when things go awry. It is a critical consideration in sound urban planning and is increasingly getting state and national attention. The impact on groundwater and other environmental assets, the scarcity of available landfill spaces, and the costs of waste transportation and disposal are increasingly focusing emphasis on solid waste management in public administration.

Management of solid waste is a critical part of a system of sustainable development. Sustainability goals tied to solid waste management include reducing the number of dangerous chemicals in soil and water, increasing the amount of recoverable waste for recycling, and lowering the amount of fossil fuel used and carbon dioxide released in transportation. Local and state governments invest growing amounts of time and financial resources to provide safe and well functioning solid waste management systems. This chapter focuses on solid waste management in public administration at both the organizational and the macrostructural levels.

Managing Solid Waste

Solid waste, by weight, is largely from packaging and containers (Rogers 2005). In the United States, about 32 percent of solid waste is discarded packaging. In addition, about 26 percent of waste is composed of nondurable goods such as paper products. About 12 percent of solid waste is composed of food scraps, 13 percent of yard trimmings, 16 percent of durable goods, and 2 percent of other types of wastes (EPA 2008a). The composition of solid waste is important to understanding the management of it. Different sustainability solutions are available for different types of waste. For instance, steel, paper products, and aluminum compose the largest amount of waste that is recycled in the United States and are currently the most effective or recoverable by-products to recycle (U.S. EPA 2008a).

There are several accepted approaches to managing solid waste. Several methods are listed and described below:

- *Landfills*. Landfills use geobarriers, constructed barriers, and leachate collectors to store wastes in a manner that prevents contaminants from reaching groundwater and soil. They are also carefully monitored for gas, which can be emitted into the atmosphere and is flammable. Landfills may store household municipal waste, construction and demolition waste, and nonhazardous industrial waste (U.S. EPA 2008b).
- *Incineration*. Incineration reduces solid waste volume through controlled burning. Filters and scrubbers are used to limit the escape of environmentally harmful materials into the atmosphere. Some solid waste incineration can be used to produce electricity.
- *Reuse*. Reuse is the use of a potential discard for another or the same purpose without running it through a resource-intensive production process. Using an old bath towel as a rag is an example of reuse. Glass milk bottles used to be regularly washed out and reused, and water cooler bottles are also often reused. Clothing has the potential for this type of reuse.
- *Recycling*. Recycling involves reclaiming the resources used in the production of a good for use in the production of the same or other products. Paper, aluminum, oil, steel, plastic, and glass are commonly recycled materials.
- *Reduction of consumption*. Reduction of consumption involves a reduction in the level of the original procurement of goods in order to reduce future waste. For instance, a person may keep a car or a pair of shoes

until they are no longer repairable or simply choose to limit purchases of luxury items.

- *Precycling.* Precycling is the selection and purchase of goods that support reduction in waste. Because packaging constitutes a great deal of solid waste discards, selecting goods with less paper and cardboard packaging would contribute to the environment through precycling.

Of the methods above, recycling has been most closely associated with environmental sustainability in the United States since the 1970s and 1980s. Media campaigns and information sharing have generally increased the recycling of solid waste (U.S. EPA 2008c). Most types of wastes are recycled effectively with the exception of steel, of which there has been a decline in the percentage recycled since the 1960s. Aluminum, motor oil, computers, glass, textiles, paper, batteries, tires, antifreeze, and plastics are among the resources regularly recycled (U.S. EPA 2008c). In addition, organic waste, such as yard trimmings, food scraps, and wood waste, is used to produce compost for gardening. Although recycling is an effective tool for sustainable development, several barriers have emerged:

- For a number of resources, the percentage of recovered products could be significantly increased. For instance, of the 85 million tons of paper discarded per year, only 52 percent is recovered, and only 11.7 percent of the 30 million tons of plastic is recovered (U.S. EPA 2008c).
- There are a number of costs to communities instituting recycling programs. Recycling programs require employees, education initiatives, storage bins, and transportation. The funds to pay for these expenses can press local budgets.
- In a number of communities, the market for certain recyclables remains underdeveloped, resulting in available recyclables, but no buyers. Often, sorted recyclables are then introduced into landfills or incinerators.
- Many citizens underestimate the efficiency gains and value in using recyclables, reducing the amount of recycling. For instance, it takes forty-five gallons of crude oil to make 2.5 quarts of motor oil, but only one gallon of used oil to make 2.5 quarts of motor oil. Also, there are significant gains in cost and environmental impact due to reduced transportation and production efforts.
- Many citizens underestimate the value of alternatives such as reuse and reduction in consumption. Although a very effective tool for reducing resource depletion, recycling still has significant costs of transportation and production. For instance, about 45 percent of soft drink and beer cans are recycled (U.S. EPA 2008c). Transporting and reformulating

the recycled aluminum for subsequent soft drink and beer distribution requires significant amounts of energy. Although aluminum recycling is one of the most efficient processes in solid waste management, it still leads to a gradual loss of resources in the long run.

Although recycling alone will not solve all the problems of solid waste management, it can significantly reduce the amount of waste entering landfills and incinerators every year. Combined with reuse, precycling, and reduced consumption, recycling has the potential to reduce negative impact on the environment and on human welfare. Public administrators must understand the situation-specific benefits and cost of all potential waste management solutions in order to introduce the best combination of solutions possible for each community.

Opportunities for Governments and Civil Society

The management of solid waste requires careful macrolevel regulation and oversight. Although coordination of waste transport may be managed privately or publicly, a number of historic lessons suggest that some government intervention is necessary. The historic impact of ocean waste dumping provides a strong example. Plastic waste outweighs zooplankton six to one in the world's oceans (Rogers 2005). From 1946 to 1972, low-level radioactive waste was regularly dumped into oceans; it required the regulation of the London Convention in 1972 and the 1993 Radwaste Disposal Ban to eliminate radioactive ocean dumping (Ringius 2001). Several laws and amendments have been adopted by the United States and the international community to reduce or eliminate the dumping of waste into ocean environments.

In the case of waste management, private players can potentially impose significant negative externalities on others. Because there is a social interest in discarding waste as cost-effectively as possible, without some government oversight and civil society intervention there is a clear threat of environmental damage to freshwater sources, oceans, land quality, and air. Governments and nonprofit organizations have an important role in ensuring that household and industrial waste does not have long-term negative consequences on the environment.

In addition to regulation and oversight, governments may need to coordinate waste management services. Because solid waste is transported between state lines, because it has impacts on multiple levels of governments, and because there are a number of private stakeholders, governments may be the best managers of large-scale environmental planning related to waste management. Further, governments may be able to provide the incentives and infrastructure to manage effective, communitywide, sustainable development projects. The following cases highlight the potential impact of this type of coordination:

- *Recycling.* In order to promote motor oil recycling, King County in Washington State now uses recycled oil for its 1,200 Metro Transit vehicles (King County 2008). In addition to using the oil in its vehicles, the county maintains a careful public record of activities and research tied to its recycled oil use.
- *Composting, recycling, and precycling.* Kamikatsu, Japan, has implemented a citywide no-waste policy. The residents of Kamikatsu sort their rubbish into more than thirty categories for recycling or composting. There is no trash pick-up service. The residents also make careful consumption and precycling choices in order to eliminate waste.
- *Electricity from incineration.* In the United States, approximately 31.4 million tons of solid waste were burned for energy recovery in 2006 (U.S. EPA 2008a). The United Kingdom burns approximately 4 million tons of solid waste annually for energy reclamation (Environmental Services Association 2006). Energy recovery and energy reclamation describe the harnessing of heat energy, previously lost in the burning process, into electricity.
- *Citizen engagement.* The Solid Waste and Financial Assistance Program in Olympia, Washington, provides citizens with extensive, detailed information on recycling and safely disposing of household waste. The program also provides incentive grants to encourage community initiatives on various waste management projects (Department of Ecology, State of Washington 2008).

All these projects, although on very different scales, involve partnerships between government and civil society to improve the management of solid waste. Governments and nonprofits also provide educational initiatives and innovation grants to communities to build capacity and infrastructure for improved environmental impact. Public administrators with technical and scientific knowledge on solid waste management have an opportunity to engage citizens in meaningful community action in order to achieve long-run positive impacts on the environment.

Agency Action to Manage Solid Waste

Individual agencies also have the power to manage their own solid waste in a sustainable manner. In fact, public and nonprofit organizations have the opportunity to model waste management decisions and actions that support

71

sustainable development for citizens and other organizations. A number of these actions have the benefit of reducing costs to the organization as well.

- *Reducing paper consumption.* The use of electronic record keeping and communication can reduce the amount of paper consumed by organizations. Using double-sided copies and recycled paper are other possibilities. Although this action may seem like a small step, it not only decreases waste but also reduces the consumption of wood, printing materials, storage space, and transportation of materials.
- *Recycling and precycling.* Many organizations recycle paper, aluminum, and glass. Those who use vehicles also may recycle tires, motor oil, and antifreeze. Green procurement policies encourage agencies to purchase recycled goods and those with the least packaging in order to contribute to a more sustainable waste management system.
- *Using ecofriendly chemicals for cleaning and construction.* The use of products with low negative environmental impact for cleaning, painting, and construction can contribute to sustainable waste management systems. The use of ecofriendly cleaning chemicals also can have benefits for freshwater systems, as these chemicals are often introduced into wastewater.
- *Reducing mailings.* Another way to reduce waste and costs is to eliminate unnecessary mailings and to combine mailings and use e-mail when possible.
- *Rebuilding and construction.* Waste from remodeling may be reduced through reuse, and recycled materials can be used in construction.
- *Food management.* Composting organic waste and using reusable containers are ways to eliminate waste.
- *Yard waste.* Using a mulching mower on green space and on leaves reduces waste and improves soil quality and water retention.

Making changes for improved waste management at the organizational level is an important responsibility of government and nonprofit organizations. The benefits are many:

- Developing and testing solutions for large-scale application in the future
- Modeling decision-making and actions to promote environmentally responsible practice by the demonstration effect of public programs
- Educating citizens and other organizations on decision and actions steps
- Potential increases in efficiency, and reduced costs to citizens and stakeholders in the long run
- Improved environmental and human well-being

- Collection and dissemination of data related to sustainable action
- Increased buy-in from external players
- Creating new markets for recycled goods, such as compost, and creating enough demand for recycling so more stations are available to citizens, thus reducing transportation costs

The innovations created on a small scale have the potential to be implemented at a larger scale in the larger community, and the information collected in public and nonprofit organizations reduces the costs of implementation for other organizations and for individuals. Combining organizational and community initiatives is likely to have strong positive impact, allowing all citizens to reap the rewards of collaboration and coordination.

Macrolevel to Microlevel Impact

As discussed in earlier chapters, sustainable development requires macrolevel and microlevel planning and action, as well as consideration of multiple overlapping systems and systems components. The relationship between solid waste management and water quality, air quality, soil quality, global climate change, and human health makes it a very important factor in sustainable development planning. For public administrators, the impact of solid waste on human populations, wildlife, and the environment requires that innovative solutions and citizen education initiatives become a part of sustainable action. Sustainable solid waste management will require technical and practical innovation as well as strong government and civil society commitment.

Questions to Consider

1. What solid waste management methods are used in the municipality or municipalities in which you work and/or reside?
2. What potential environmentally sustainable waste management methods could be implemented in your community? In your organization?
3. Waste incineration reduces solid waste volume and can be used to produce energy. Do these benefits outweigh the potential costs to air quality and global climate change through emissions?
4. Discuss the roles of citizens, nonprofit organizations, governments, and private business in managing solid waste and its environmental impacts.

8

Transportation

Transportation is critical to the effort of achieving sustainability. A great deal of air and water pollution is produced by cars, planes, trains, and other vehicles that use internal combustion engines. These engines also consume a large amount of the world's petroleum, which is in finite supply. Yet the desire to travel among people all over the world is strong, so there are few signs of abating the demand for petroleum and its consequent pollution. What can be done?

A variety of approaches have been suggested. New vehicles that pollute less are being developed, and other technological changes offer some promise. Economic approaches such as applying new user charges to driving and flying offer hope. Maybe people could reduce their travel if cities were designed better and good mass transportation alternatives were made available. These approaches are part of the solution. In addition, we believe that a concerted effort to change policies and how they are implemented is necessary. The fundamental problem is that the economic incentives and the political structure do not support a sustainable approach to transportation. This situation needs to change.

This chapter applies sustainability to transportation by applying the four dimensions of sustainability discussed in Chapter 2: environmental, economic, financial, and social. It identifies the problems along these dimen-

This chapter is adapted with permission from Sage Publications from the following articles: John R. Bartle, "The sustainable development of U.S. air transportation: The promise and challenge of institutional reform," *Public Works Management & Policy* 10, 3 (2006): 214–224; and John R. Bartle and Jijesh Devan, "Sustainable highways: Destination or mirage?" *Public Works Management & Policy* 10, 3 (2006): 225–234.

sions principally applied to highway and air transportation, then examines current policies, and then discusses four proposed approaches to reform: pollution control policies, technological improvement, reduced use, and taxation. The last section discusses the potential to change institutions and suggests an integrated set of policies and institutional changes for long-term reform.

Sustainability in Transportation

An environmentally sustainable transportation system has been defined as "one where transportation does not endanger public health or ecosystems and meets the needs for access consistent with (1) use of renewable resources below their rates of regeneration, and (2) use of non-renewable resources below the rates of development of renewable substitutes" (UNESCAP, 2001, 11). A third condition that has been added is that "the rate of pollution emissions does not exceed the assimilative capacity of the environment" (Black 2004). Put more simply, the broad goal is to balance the desire for mobility with the use of resources. Another definition of sustainable transport is the provision of the same level of transport and mobility with nondeclining values of total capital (Black 2004). As discussed in Chapter 2, declining total capital leads to a long-term decrease in wealth and income.

The four dimensions of sustainability identified in Chapter 2 as applied to transportation are as follows:

- *Environmental:* Limiting the use of natural capital to levels that can be replaced by natural regeneration.
- *Economic:* Achieving the highest social return on physical and natural capital. Transportation is not an end in itself; it is a means to an end, and if resources are used wastefully, the means are inefficient.
- *Financial:* Attracting sufficient funds to cover all costs over the long term.
- *Social:* Balancing the consumption of natural capital with improvements in the standard of living and the quality of life—in particular, poverty reduction. Specifically, this dimension emphasizes providing access for the poor to the transportation network and ensuring equity in service provision.

The development of sustainable transportation ideally balances the demand for mobility with the natural resources used up in providing them, while correcting for market failures, balancing finances, and achieving social equity goals. Forecasts of transportation demand suggest that it will be hard to achieve the goal of environmental sustainability. World highway travel is forecasted to increase rapidly, doubling from 1990 to 2020 and then doubling again by 2050 (Schafer and Victor 1997). World air passenger traffic is projected to increase by over 250 percent from 2002 to 2022, and world airfreight transport will grow even faster (Whitelegg and Cambridge 2004). Without major improvements in technology, these forecasts mean that the use of fossil fuel will increase to clearly unsustainable levels.

Environmental

The main environmental problems caused by transportation are emissions, noise, injuries, and deaths. Emissions have impacts at both the global and local levels. Vehicles, planes, and locomotives emit greenhouse gases (carbon dioxide and nitrous oxides) that are one of the causes of global warming. Nitrous oxides also contribute to smog and acid rain (Dempsey 2000). Cars and trucks are the largest source of carbon monoxide in the United States and significant producers of volatile organic compounds (BTS 2003a). Although airplanes are responsible for only a small portion of greenhouse gas emissions, because these emissions are injected at high levels in the atmosphere, they have three times the impact on global warming than emissions on the ground level (NRC 2003; Whitelegg and Cambridge 2004).

Emissions also have local effects that damage the health of commuters and those living near highways and airports. Nearly half of all Americans live with unhealthy levels of air pollution (Ernst, Corless, and Greene-Roesel 2003). Research has linked air pollution to a host of public health concerns, including asthma, cancer, heart disease, heart attack, stroke, high blood pressure, birth defects, and brain damage (American Lung Association 2002).

A by-product of transportation is noise, which also is associated with health problems, specifically cardiovascular disease, impaired hearing, depression, irritability, chronic tinnitus, and sleep disturbance (Dempsey 2000). The health effects are even more acute for children, who suffer from increased heart rates, increased stress, impaired attention span and memory function, and impaired reading performance (Whitelegg and Cambridge 2004). Noise effects near airports have been estimated to reduce property values by about 0.6 percent per decibel (NRC 2003).

Another obvious health effect is injuries and deaths caused by travel and provision of transportation. As Black writes, it "should be an accepted premise that a transport system that kills off its users is not sustainable" (2004, 12). In 2006, there were 44,912 transportation-related fatalities in the United States,

---

An Unsustainable Supply Chain

The just-in-time inventory policy of some retail businesses is beneficial to consumers in many ways, as it delivers goods quickly without the costs of warehousing. But when freight transport is not charged for the costs of pollution, it can become an unsustainable practice. Garments made in Korea, for example, are flown overnight to New York for sale in retail outlets the next day. The jet that flies in the goods produces twenty times more carbon dioxide per ton-kilometer than would a truck transporting the same goods from North Carolina, and the difference in mileage is more than ten times, resulting in an increase in greenhouse gas emissions by over 200 times. Yet none of the environmental costs of transporting the goods are reflected in the price of the garments. Because the cost of the environmental capacity used to deliver these goods is not paid by the producers or consumers, natural capital is wasted, and there may be an inappropriate relocation of the manufacturing activity; thus "the market price ignores the social cost of production" (Dempsey 2000, 686).

---

the vast majority on the highways (BTS 2008). Also, many animals are killed on highways, on runways, and by planes in flight.

Economic

One of the fundamental ironies of transportation is that the negative externalities caused by transportation are subsidized although economic theory would recommend instead that they be taxed. In the United States, all modes of transportation are directly and indirectly subsidized yet people complain that there is too much traffic, pollution, and noise. The social costs of highway transportation due to congestion, traffic delays, accidents, roadway damage, land use, and other side effects have been estimated by Miller and Moffet at over a trillion dollars (1993). Clearly, then, policies subsidizing transportation that create these high social costs need to be reformed.

As the box above illustrates, part of the sustainability problem is caused by incorrect economic incentives. The absence of an appropriate price signal for the use of environmental capacity can lead to wasting natural capital. Public policies should correct market failures by making travel bear the full costs, which would foster genuine competition between all modes of travel, improve land use, and increase access by clustering business and residential areas together.

According to the World Business Council for Sustainable Development

(WBCSD), a coalition of about 200 international corporations drawn from thirty-five nations, "for all our companies, long run success depends on the future viability of mobility. It is our collective view that the mobility sector will not be healthy over the long term unless mobility is made sustainable" (WBCSD 2004, 6).

Financial

Financial incentives in U.S. transportation financing are problematic in several ways. First, the fuel taxes that have historically financed American highways are increasingly being replaced by local general revenue sources (Wachs 2003), which means that general tax dollars are subsidizing driving. Second, highway taxes do not reflect the costs of damage to pavement or the cost of congestion. Therefore they provide the wrong incentives to drivers and road builders, wasting resources and creating premature obsolescence of roads (Small, Winston, and Evans 1989). Third, motor fuel taxes, airline ticket taxes, and flight segment taxes are the main source of revenue for the highway and airport and airway trust funds. Rather than using these taxes as a tool to discourage travel and the resulting pollution, the revenues from the taxes are used for construction that often promotes more travel.

Fourth, air transportation fees are poorly designed to achieve sustainability goals. Airport landing fees are generally assessed based on aircraft weight; however, aircraft weight is not well correlated with emissions. Airlines and other aircraft operators therefore do not have an incentive to reduce emissions, leading to more flights causing more air pollution. Similarly, passenger facility charges (PFC) allow airports to charge each enplaned passenger up to $4.50, with funds used to supplement grants to airports and debt repayment. PFCs do not create a close link between the costs of the projects they fund and the benefits received by the passengers paying for them. Further, they are assessed on a per passenger basis, despite the fact that an empty plane pollutes almost as much as a full plane. Again, these fees do not appropriately charge travelers for the value of the resources they are using, leading to wasteful consumption. Finally, the structure of federal aid for highways and airports generally uses predetermined matching rates in distributing funds. These matching rates tend to be too high with overly restrictive rules regarding use of funds (Gramlich 1994), thus leading to building too much of certain types of infrastructure and too little of other types. The Intermodal Surface Transportation Efficiency Act of 1991 (ISTEA) stimulated the examination and application of flexible matching grant programs and congestion pricing under the value-pricing program, which is a step in the right direction.

Social

Social equity concerns in transportation are focused on access, congestion relief, health, and the effects of noise and pollution on different populations. The WBCSD (2004) calls for a narrowing of the gap between the poorest and richest nations and between the poor and the middle class within nations. This step would enhance the access of the poor to mobility, although it may do so at the expense of higher traffic levels. The Bureau of Transportation Statistics indicates that the working poor in the United States spend nearly 10 percent of their income on commuting expenses. The working poor who drive to work pay even more, an average of 21 percent of their income in commuting expenses, four times that of the median percentage for a person commuting by car (BTS 2003b). Compared to other groups in society, more of the working poor uses other modes to commute; still, 66 percent of the working poor drive and so face a heavy expense simply to get to work. Thus, for some, access to transportation for commuting is expensive and difficult. In part, this is the result of the physical structure of cities where it is difficult to get to certain places without a car.

Noise and emissions tend to have disproportionate effects on the poor, with the greatest harm done to those working and living near highways and airports. As mentioned, children, a relatively powerless group, are more adversely affected than adults, an imbalance that exacerbates intergenerational equity.

This section shows that transportation generally does not meet the goals of sustainability. Many solutions have been suggested. The next section evaluates these solutions.

Current Pollution Control Policies

Several laws and international agreements contribute to the goal of sustainability. The two most important pieces of legislation are the Kyoto Protocol and ISTEA. In 1997 the Kyoto Protocol set goals for reductions in the emissions of carbon dioxide, methane, and nitrous oxides 2012. This protocol has been ratified or acceded to by more than 140 nations, with the notable exception of the United States. However, international aviation emissions are excluded from the Kyoto Protocol, in part because of the difficulty of apportioning the responsibility to reduce these emissions. The result is a classic example of the problem of common pool goods, resulting in the "tragedy of the commons." Because there is no governing body with sufficient power, there is no incentive to reduce emissions.

ISTEA declares the policy of the U.S. government to develop a transportation system that is "economically efficient and environmentally sound while moving individuals and property in an energy efficient way" (Benfield and Replogle 2002, 10638). ISTEA emphasizes multimodal solutions to achieve a wide variety of goals, such as developing advanced vehicle programs for fuel efficiency, increasing alternate forms of mobility, and emphasizing health, environmental quality, equity, and aesthetic and cultural values (Horan, Dittmar, and Jordan 1999, 218). ISTEA allows the states to use funding for new programs that would mitigate traffic congestion, increase safety, and contribute to the attainment of air quality standards and also mandates specific steps to open up the transportation planning process to the public. ISTEA also has effective implementation tools to ensure that transportation projects would be sensitive to the environment. Different programs prioritize air quality improvement, community enhancement projects, and metropolitan planning (Schweppe 2001).

In air travel, another important policy instrument is the United Nations' International Civil Aviation Organization (ICAO), the legal authority that drafts treaties and agreements related to air law. In 1993 the ICAO amended aircraft standards to reduce nitrous oxides emissions by 20 percent, and in 1999 it lowered allowable emissions by another 16 percent (Dempsey 2000). However, according to Button, the ICAO has "limited powers to enforce even the measures that may be needed to fully embrace global environmental factors into international policies" (2004, 20).

The most important pieces of legislation in the United States that support sustainable air travel are the following:

- The National Environmental Policy Act of 1969, which created the environmental assessment and environmental impact statement processes.
- The Noise Control Act of 1972, which gave the Environmental Protection Agency (EPA) and the Federal Aviation Administration (FAA) a role in formulating aircraft noise standards.
- The Aviation Safety and Noise Abatement Act of 1979, which gave the EPA and the FAA jurisdiction to monitor and regulate aircraft noise and emissions.
- The Airport Noise and Capacity Act of 1990, which required a phase-out of old aircraft that were noisy and emitted high levels of pollution.

The roles and duties of federal agencies are also important. The National Aeronautic and Space Administration (NASA) is the only federal agency conducting research on commercial aviation pollution. NASA also takes the lead in research on aircraft noise. The FAA has programs concerned with noise regulation and aircraft certification, and the EPA is responsible for enforcing emissions and noise standards. NASA's goals are to reduce noise levels by

75 percent by 2022 (compared to 1997 levels), carbon dioxide by 50 percent, and nitrogen oxide by 80 percent. However, the National Research Council has found that the current level of funding for federal research is too low to achieve this goal on schedule (NRC 2003, 15, 33).

In the area of surface travel, the key legislation is the following:

- The Federal Aid Highway Act of 1962, which mandated the use of an integrated transportation planning process for highway construction by relating land use to social and community values (Horan, Dittmar, and Jordan 1999).
- The Federal Aid Highway Act of 1968, which mandated public hearings and citizen participation for highway projects, as well as assistance for people displaced by highways.
- The Clean Air Act of 1970, which created emission standards leading to national ambient air quality standards (Horan, Dittmar, and Jordan 1999); the Clean Air Act of 1977, which instituted sanctions against noncompliance with air quality standards; and the Clean Air Act of 1990, which strengthened these regulations and emission standards.

While substantial progress has been made over the last forty years toward sustainability goals, the current structure of laws and agency powers still leaves transportation short of a sustainable path of development.

Technology

Historically, technology has reduced the pollution caused by motor vehicles and airplanes, a trend that is expected to continue. The efficiency of the internal combustion engine can be increased and conventional and greenhouse gas emissions can be reduced by employing hybrid-electric powertrain. Hydrogen-based proton exchange membrane fuel cells offer the promise of even greater reductions in emissions, but there are problems with weight, cost, availability, and the distribution and storage of hydrogen (Truett 2004; NRC 2003). Other features that can increase the sustainability of automobiles are improved technology to lessen the weight of vehicles, improved aerodynamics to reshape the automobile body, and technologies to reduce rolling resistance. For aircraft, fuel efficiency has been improved by advances in engine technology, airframe design, and operations. It is estimated that future improvements in technology can reduce fuel consumption of airplanes by 1 percent per revenue-passenger-kilometer annually over the next fifteen to twenty years. However, the projections are that commercial traffic will increase by 3 to 5 percent over the same period, overwhelming the technological gains.

Congestion Charges in London

In February 2003, London, England, implemented a congestion pricing policy for each vehicle (excepting specific exempted vehicles) entering the central business area on weekdays. The charge, initially about $7 in U.S. currency, was increased to $11.23 in July 2005. The most recent report by Transport for London (2007) indicates that the policy has been successful:

- Car and truck traffic in the charging zone was 21 percent less, reducing congestion and travel times.
- Many car users switched to the bus and to cycling; fewer drivers appear to have switched to the underground (subway).
- The impact on retail trade, hospitality businesses, and the financial service sector has been positive.
- Road traffic accidents and injuries have been reduced.
- Emissions have been reduced.
- In 2006–2007 the policy generated $173 million, which was principally spent on improvements in bus service.
- A cost-benefit analysis found a favorable benefit-to-cost ratio of 1.5 when the charge was $7, increasing to 1.7 when the charge increased to $11.23.

Technology also has made important historical advances in reducing the noise of airplanes. Technological changes, phasing out old aircraft, and operations improvements have made aircraft quieter by an estimated three decibels per decade over the past forty years. While traffic increased by a factor of six from 1975 to 2000, the number of people affected by noise in the United States fell by a factor of fifteen as a result of technological improvements. However, further reductions are expected to be small because the fleet is relatively new and no phase-outs of aircraft are anticipated (NRC 2003). Highway noise pollution also can be reduced by improved tire technology, as tire noise is the biggest contributor to highway noise.

Reduced Use

Over time, federal policies have been based on the belief that new technology could make cars cleaner, more efficient, and safer without the disruption of limiting driving (Leone 1999). However, as economic growth has increased car ownership and urban sprawl, it is becoming clear that sustainability goals are unlikely to be attained if economic growth cannot be decoupled from automobile use. There are some indications of movement away from car dependence. The private sector is endorsing ways to reduce car dependence by strengthening multimodal planning processes and expanding commuter benefit programs (Association for Commuter Transportation 2002). In other nations, there is less tolerance of the unsustainable effects of cars. Singapore levies heavy taxes on cars, auctions the right to buy cars, and imposes high fees for downtown driving. Denmark has banned cars in phases from central business districts to wean citizens away from dependence on their vehicles (Hawken, Lovins, and Lovins 1999), while London has imposed a congestion charge on auto and truck travel in the central business area that has been successful.

The goal of mobility may always conflict to some degree with sustainability. However, it is possible to reduce some low-priority travel. As Wachs (2004) points out, American attitudes have been changed by public education efforts in numerous areas: reduced smoking, increased recycling, reduced drinking and driving, and the promotion of safe sex; it is possible that similar educational campaigns could reduce low-priority travel.

Another solution is to travel by modes that pollute less. For example, the emission of carbon dioxide caused by airplanes is much greater than the same per-person-kilometer travel by other modes. Dempsey writes that carbon dioxide emission by planes "is between four and eight times that of travel by automobile, more than ten times that of travel by bus, and twenty-two times that of electric-powered train" (2000, 653–654). For freight travel, these magnitudes are even larger: twenty times that of truck travel and 240 times that of rail. To shift traffic among the modes, financial or regulatory incentives are probably necessary.

Taxing the Externalities

The problems of air pollution, noise, congestion, and greenhouse gases caused by transportation are negative externalities. Economists have long argued that these externalities need to be internalized in order to achieve an efficient allocation of goods and services. The United Nations Economic and Social Commission for Asia and the Pacific (2001, 56) concluded that "the internalization of externalities is a fundamental requirement in devising transport pricing policies to promote sustainable development." One approach to do so is to tax the externality; others are regulation and reassignment of property rights. Internalizing external costs would alleviate these problems and produce revenue that could be used for mitigation expenses. Further, if modes and vehicles that pollute more than others face the highest taxes, this will stimulate a shift to less-polluting vehicles. According to the United Kingdom

Royal Commission on Environmental Pollution, "the demand for air transport might not be growing at the present rate if airlines and their customers had to face the costs of the damage they are causing to the environment (1994, 75). "Tax reforms that move toward correct pricing of goods and services are therefore an attractive tool to improve sustainability.

Kyoto Protocol signatories are using regulation and taxes as a way to meet their targets by either reducing greenhouse gases or enhancing carbon sinks or both. Carbon sinks are reservoirs that accumulate carbon. They may be natural (such as oceans or soil) or man-made (such as "carbon capture and storage" industrial processes which re-engineer stationary pollution sources such as factories to reduce their carbon emissions). The European Union, which has articulated the principle that polluters should pay for their environmental damage, has adopted a policy of tariffs on airport infrastructure, and taxes and duties on trucks (Whitelegg and Cambridge 2004). A variety of pollution charges have been suggested for air transport: emission charges, landing and takeoff emission charges, fuel charges, and ticket charges (Bleijenberg and Wit 1998). Brockhagen and Lienemeyer (1999) have determined the level of emissions charges that would be necessary to reduce global warming to achieve the standards of the Kyoto Protocol. For a one-way flight from London Heathrow to New York on a Boeing 747–400 with 310 passengers, this charge would amount to a total of €28,764, or €92.8 per passenger, about $117 at current (2009) exchange rates. This is a substantial increase that would be of questionable political practicality, despite its economic merits.

The strategy of charging for pollution and congestion is only beginning to be implemented in Europe and is used only sparingly in the United States. There are several reasons why this solution has not been pursued: technological difficulties, legal challenges, political acceptability (by both general and specific publics), and concerns about economic competitiveness. In addition, the complexity of the administrative and intergovernmental channels through which transportation is delivered makes it difficult to implement pricing policies. In short, institutions are designed to serve other goals besides economic efficiency. However, institutions do change over time in response to social and political pressures, and such a change can happen here. Ubbels and Verhoef (2005) point to some lessons that have been learned about the adoption of pricing policies:

- There needs to be a sense of fairness about the charges.
- The plan needs to be perceived as effective in reducing congestion, saving traveling time, and improving reliability.
- The plan needs to be communicated effectively to the affected groups, and major stakeholders need to accept the solution.
- The use of the revenue generated by charges needs to be equitable. This

goal is most likely to be achieved when the funds are used to improve roads, mass transit, or other parts of the transportation system, thus decreasing delays and congestion.

Despite these institutional challenges, there are attractive opportunities. A study of a congestion pricing proposal in southern California (Small 1992) found that a policy could be crafted that would make every class of traveler better off, thus reducing opposition. This sort of crafting of institutions is part of the solution to the problem of unsustainable transportation, as is discussed further below.

Institutional Reform

The limitations of the solutions presented above suggest a more fundamental need to reform the institutions that have led us to this situation. Current policy has created a structure of institutions and incentives that is the more fundamental cause of unsustainability in transportation. This structure cannot be changed with one single action, but needs to be recast in a way that will reinforce progress toward the goal of sustainability. According to the WBCSD, "moving towards sustainable mobility will involve paying as much attention to institutional frameworks as to the inherent potential of any vehicle technology or fuel or the theoretical 'effectiveness' or 'ineffectiveness' of any particular policy lever or action" (2004, 27).

Institutional barriers to sustainability include the following:

- The Kyoto Protocol does not include international aviation emissions in its limits, and the United States and other nations are not party to the agreement.
- International agreements on taxation prohibit taxing fuel for international flights.
- Research and development leading to pollution reduction may be too costly for businesses in industries with low profit margins.
- Free or subsidized parking encourages commuters to drive rather than to use public transit, allowing them to live farther away from their workplace and transit lines and thus causing urban sprawl, which makes public transit more expensive to provide.

A major change like sustainability that affects so many dimensions of people's lives cannot be woven into the fabric of a nation's institutions quickly or easily. Further, the holistic emphasis of sustainability requires that it integrate across policy areas, which is especially challenging in a political system with divided powers, like that of the United States. However, the European Union (EU) is an example of a federation that has transformed its institutions

---

Cleaning the Air in Delhi

Recently, an ordinance adopted in Delhi, India, required all public buses and taxis to use liquefied petroleum gas. While the ordinance was quickly effective and very popular, achieving it took several years of debate and weeks of public demonstrations by taxi and motorized rickshaw owners and operators. The shift did not require new technology or reduced mobility. Rather, it required a change in law and the enforcement power to make it stick. As Stough and Rietveld write, "there can be little doubt that the primary barriers to sustainable transport are institutional" (2005, 1).

---

to embrace sustainability (Connor and Dovers 2004). The concept is embedded in the EU constitution, which establishes a legally enforceable commitment to sustainable policies, such as granting legal standing to those harmed by pollution. This is an example of an institutional feature that supports the goal of sustainability and will continue to reinforce it over time.

Connor and Dovers (2004) suggest two approaches that benefit from the institutional insight: strategic environmental assessment (SEA) and property rights instruments (PRI). Following the logic of environmental impact statements, SEA systematically evaluates the environmental consequences of policy, weighing them equally with economic and social concerns. It can enter at various phases of the process: planning, policy formulation, legislative consideration, and cumulative assessment. SEA has been implemented fully or partially in several countries in Europe and the British Commonwealth. PRI establishes entitlements to resource use, such as the capture of value from these rights and the ability to trade them. Property rights may be identified for various elements of resource use: access, withdrawal, management, exclusion, and alienation (the right to sell or lease the resource). Both of these approaches could be applied to local emissions problems and noise pollution.

Despite the complexities of creating a comprehensive solution to a global problem, there are examples of successful implementation. Connor and Dovers (2004) detail the evolution of environmental policy in the EU, showing how institutional structure can be changed in a complex federal system. The key features they identify are (1) a reiterative framework, in which principles, policies, and implementation procedures are regularly revisited and revised as appropriate, (2) the use of formal and informal networks that involve a variety of actors on a number of levels, and (3) a combination of both top-down and bottom-up processes of political change. These features foster an integrated set of policies, in which environmental policy is not seen as separate from other policies, policies are matched with the appropriate level of government, and political and bureaucratic capacity is stable and promotes continued policy learning. While the United States has not achieved this level of advancement in sustainable development, the EU example shows one way that it can be achieved. To accomplish this goal in the United States would require doing so in a way consistent with its political, economic, social, and cultural institutions.

Sustainable transportation policy will maximize the wealth possible from all forms of capital. Incentives that waste any form of capital lead to lower long-term growth and a lower future quality of life. Achieving this efficiency will not be done by a single policy approach because different institutional structures create different costs and incentives. Some current policies, such as the environmental impact statement process and the subsidization of research and development in emissions and noise reduction, have moved in this direction. The critical next steps are to examine the details of these administrative processes with an eye to improving efficiency and equity, making transportation more sustainable in the long run.

No single approach will solve these complex, global problems. However, a variety of reforms have been suggested, providing a starting point on the path toward a more sustainable transportation system. Generally, these reforms call for correcting the structure of incentives to reflect the full value of all capital assets. This incentive structure is an artifact of the current institutional structure. Institutional reform is therefore central to the goal of using resources efficiently. While some of these reforms go against long-standing policies, in an era of increasingly scarce resources they provide an alternate approach to achieving sustainable transportation. Eliminating wasteful and destructive incentives in conjunction with technological improvements would reduce global warming and increase the contribution of transportation to economic growth.

Questions to Consider

1. Would you be willing to pay a $117 emission tax for a flight from New York to London? If not, how much would you pay? What does this imply about the acceptability of externality taxes?
2. Is hydrogen fuel cell technology becoming a feasible replacement for the internal combustion engine? What are the positives and negatives of this technology?
3. How do most people at your office or on your campus commute? What are the barriers to more widespread use of sustainable transit? Sketch out an action plan to get more of your colleagues to commute in a sustainable way.

9

Wildlife and Oceans

At a conference on public administration in 2006 an audience member made an interesting comment during a presentation on sustainable development in public administration: "If this is about some three-toed frog going extinct, I don't want to hear about it," he said. His comment was meant to suggest that public administration should be concerned about practical applications of sustainability that have direct impacts on human beings. However, a three-toed frog could indeed indicate an important and relevant impact on human life. Frogs not only control insect populations and provide skin toxins for medical use, but also are an indicator species. Mutations and mortality in frogs, for instance, can indicate diminishing water and soil quality. Frogs generally have five toes on each of their hind legs and four fingers on each arm. A three-toed sloth or a three-toed box turtle is okay, but a three-toed frog is a mutant. Mutations leading to extra or missing appendages, as well as changes in the reproductive system, can be caused by pesticides and pollution that could also harm humans. In addition, species of frogs, along with newts, toads, and salamanders, are at risk of extinction due to the spread of chytrid fungus, which may have been introduced to global wild populations through the pet trade. Frogs, therefore, along with the thousands of other species in the environment, are tied to sustainable public administration practice in a way that the conference attendee overlooked. Public and nongovernmental organizations across the world work to protect ecosystems, sometimes by focusing on a single critical species and sometimes by addressing problems that place the entire system at risk.

The number of nonprofit and public organizations working to conserve wildlife and oceans attests to the relevance of sustainable development in public administration. Public and nonprofit agencies manage day-to-day interaction between humans and wildlife, dealing with the potential conflicts caused by increased human resource demands and development on the environment. A number of human behaviors impact the sustainability of the natural environment and the welfare of human, animal, and plant populations:

• *Development*. The use of land and other resources for residential, business, and industrial development can result in conflict and competition between humans and indigenous species (Dizard 1999). Outcomes include the elimination of wildlife species from developed properties and the destruction of habitat. The invasion of developed properties by indigenous animals also can pose health and safety risks to both human and animal life: for example, geese in parks or on public beaches, bears in housing developments, and crocodiles in swimming pools.

• *Increases in human population*. The increase in the number of human individuals can lead to use of natural resources at levels higher than the carrying capacity of the environment, resulting in negative outcomes for humans and wildlife (Dizard 1999). The overfishing of fish species is an example. A species many be vulnerable because it is overtargeted as a food source or because it is a bycatch of fishing for food species.

• *Agriculture*. The use of land for agriculture and the use of pesticides and fertilizers can negatively impact indigenous species. Examples include the impact of pesticides on amphibian and fish reproduction and the potential accidental release of bioengineered species into ecosystems. For instance, the release of nutrients into ocean water from agriculture has resulted in a large increase in the population of the crown-of-thorns starfish in Australia's Great Barrier Reef. The increased population causes enormous damage to coral, which is a primary food source for the starfish.

• *Deforestation*. Deforestation involves the removal of large plots of plant species, which can result in the destruction of ecosystems and habitat. Soil quality diminishes as organic materials are removed, and erosion is a potential problem. Slash-and-burn processes introduce carbon emissions into the environment and contribute to global climate change. In Alberta, Canada, for instance, oil sand development has caused extensive damage to forest ecosystems. Although regulations require replanting of stripped areas, recovery is made difficult by habitat destruction and removal of mature trees from the ecosystem. A similar example is the damage caused by logging and agricultural development in the rain forests of Brazil.

• *Pet trading and introduced species*. The selling of endangered and vulnerable animals in the pet trade can harm the long-term viability of that species and of its indigenous ecosystem. The removal of cornerstone species—

species that provide a resource base for other species—can have significant negative outcomes on the remainder of wildlife. The addition of introduced or exotic species into an environment can also have negative impacts. Maryland's Department of Natural Resources is currently battling the northern snakehead fish, a Chinese species with the potential to harm other native fish populations. Another introduced species, the dandelion, prompts the use of numerous gallons of weed killers on U.S. lawns each year.

Human actions have a great deal of impact on ecological systems. Mass extinction of wildlife species can result from volcanic activity, asteroid crashes, disease, climate change, and rises in sea level, but environmentally unsustainable human activities also have the potential to bring about mass extinction (Ellis 2004). In addition, human contributions to global climate change, the rise in sea level, and the spread of disease potentially magnify naturally occurring changes. However, human beings also have the potential to positively impact wildlife and oceans, and thousands of organizations work to conserve wildlife species and natural environments. The remainder of this chapter will present the roles of nonprofit and public agencies in wildlife and ocean management and sustainability.

The Role of Nonprofit and Public Agencies in Ocean and Wildlife Sustainability

Nonprofit and public organizations provide an enormous amount of support for wildlife and ocean sustainability. The International Union for Conservation of Nature (IUCN), a global network of organizations devoted to research and action tied to species conservation, is one example. The IUCN has 872 international and national nongovernment organizations and 195 government organizations as members (IUCN 2008). Member organizations include the U.S. Department of State, Bureau of Oceans and International Environmental and Scientific Affairs, the National Geographic Society, the National Audubon Society, the Sierra Club, the International Association of Fish and Wildlife Agencies, and Conservation International. The work of the organization includes management of the "Red List," a research-driven database identifying at-risk wildlife species. In addition, the network provides resources for the improvement of human and wildlife welfare. As a collaborative of both public and nonprofit organizations, the IUCN demonstrates the interrelationship of duties and responsibilities for both types of agencies. As an international network, it demonstrates the need for global collaboration in sustainable development planning and action.

Nonprofit and government organizations provide many types of services tied to wildlife and ocean sustainability. Some services are designed for very specific species or local impacts; others have system-wide, global, and multispecies impact. Some of the types of services and resources provided are described below:

- *Conservation.* Organizations work to preserve natural habitats and resources, to reduce the negative impact of human-influenced and naturally occurring variables on wildlife species, and to ensure the long-term viability of species. An example is the conservation of Gombe River National Park in Tanzania and the related protection of chimpanzees living in the region by the Jane Goodall Institute.
- *Advocacy.* Organizations work to change human actions, laws, and infrastructures through the use of tools such as lobbying, education, and marketing. The creation of the United Nations Convention on International Trade in Endangered Species and Wild Fauna and Flora (CITES) is an example of advocacy by IUCN. It is an international agreement protecting over 30,000 species. The work of the National Audubon Society in advocacy related to the 1973 Endangered Species Act is another example.
- *Research.* Organizations build knowledge to guide action regarding wildlife and ocean management and sustainability. The U.S. Geological Survey maintains weather and geographic data that can be used for sustainability planning. In addition, it supports a number of "biological partnerships" with organizations such as the Nature Conservancy and the Wildlife Management Institute to build research in the field.
- *Education.* Organizations provide information, knowledge, training, and opportunities for experiential learning to citizens. The Association of Zoos and Aquariums, an accrediting body for zoos and aquariums, has a membership of over 200 organizations whose driving goals are education, animal care, and conservation.
- *Funding.* Organizations also raise or collect money for wildlife and ocean management. Governments collect taxes, fees, and fines; nonprofits collect donations and fees and do extensive fund-raising. Both types of organizations may provide grants or resource support to other organizations. An example is the work of the Nature Conservancy, which does fund-raising to purchase large tracts of land for conservation purposes. The World Wildlife Fund raises funds for protection of nineteen major conservation regions and also offers scholarships and fellowships.
- *Laws, rules, and regulations.* Organizations provide information and research documents to political decision-makers on issues impacting wildlife and oceans. Government organizations also coordinate agency

rule-making, administer laws, and oversee compliance with regulations. In addition, organizations may provide information to citizens on how to participate in rule-making and regulation development. For example, the U.S. Environmental Protection Agency provides citizens with information on how to access laws, rules, and regulations and how to become involved in decision-making.

- *Coordination.* Organizations also act to coordinate services and resources for wildlife conservation. For instance, the U.S. Fish and Wildlife Service regularly coordinates wildlife conservation efforts with Native American tribes and private and public landowners. It also maintains information on laws and policies and runs the nation's endangered species program. Another example is the Plant Conservation Alliance, a network of ten governments and over 270 private partners, which coordinates native plant conservation and habitat restoration in the United States.

- *Planning.* Organizations may coordinate planning for regional conservation efforts or to manage specific environmental problems. For example, Alaska's Division of Wildlife Conservation maintains a statewide strategic plan for wildlife management and also creates species-specific plans. This multitier planning is used and documented by a number of state and provincial governments across the world. The U.S. Fish and Wildlife Service coordinates habitat conservation plans (HCPs), which are permits designed to protect endangered wildlife species from human activities and development. The HCP requires permit applicants to offset harmful impacts of human activities on endangered wildlife and to formally document the plan.

- *Prevention of cruelty.* Organizations provide protection from cruelty to animal species. One example is American Humane, an organization that uses education, advocacy, and research to protect the interests of children and animals. The Humane Society of the United States also has a mission of animal protection. It provides services and resources to prevent cruelty to pets, farm animals, wildlife, horses used in racing, and animals used in research.

- *Economics.* Organizations provide research, education, and resources to mitigate negative impacts on wildlife as a result of human poverty, as well as support of economic development. Examples include education provided by the U.S. Department of Agriculture, the Natural Conservation Service, and the research- and market-based education and advocacy of Defenders of Wildlife.

- *Rights.* Organizations seek to promote rights for nonhuman species. The ethical stance can range from assigning basic legal protections for animal species to supporting the establishment of rights equivalent to the rights of human populations. An example of an organization working on this issue is the Humane Society of the United States.

- *Recreation.* Organizations that depend upon wildlife resources for human recreational benefit include nonprofit and government zoos, parks, and aquariums, which provide opportunities for human and wildlife interaction (Davis 1997; Hanson 2002). Education is often combined with the recreational value of this interaction.

The examples above only touch on the extensive work of nonprofit and public organizations working on wildlife- and ocean-focused sustainable development in public administration. The work of these agencies is especially relevant because of the relationship between wildlife species and natural resource welfare. Water quality and quantity, air quality, soil quality, biodiversity, global climate change, disease management, and food security are all related to wildlife and ocean sustainability. Further, the field sees overlapping economic, political, religious, historical, and legal interests at work (Wise 2002). Strong civil society and public administration commitments make it one of the most interesting and complex areas in sustainable development.

Citizens, Science, and Solutions

Sustainable solutions in wildlife and ocean management require both scientific, technology-based action and also changes in human behavior. This is why research and education are a regular function of organizations working in the field. A difficulty in all sustainable development projects is the balancing of citizen engagement or participation and the use of technical and scientific knowledge in decision-making. Because species protection is tied to local and regional decisions and actions, it is necessary for public administrators to obtain the support and commitment of citizens. Several related factors must be considered:

- Citizens must be able to access, understand, and apply scientific and technical information. Information may need to be presented in several formats and with the use of different tools for differing audiences.
- Citizens must have the decision-making power and tools to achieve sustainable behavior and the resources to carry out related action.
- Human poverty and economic needs must be addressed concurrently with wildlife needs.
- Laws, regulations, rules, and incentives must be meaningful for changing negative human behaviors and for supporting positive behaviors.
- Conflicting scientific and technical knowledge must be responsibly translated and coordinated in order to support decision-making.

Nonprofit and public agencies have the opportunity to create long-term solutions for species conservation using sustainable development planning and assessment tools. Their contribution also includes building a base of research and knowledge, translating that information for citizen decision-making, and facilitating planning that considers human and environmental well being in the long run.

Questions to Consider

1. Wildlife and ocean sustainability is tied to many other components of sustainable development in public administration. Discuss the relevance of these systems relationships.
2. In Chapter 3 of this book, the concept of rights for nonhumans was discussed. What legal protections and/or rights should be available to nonhuman species? Discuss the difference between legal protections and rights as they apply to the issue.
3. Explore specific nonprofit and government agencies working on wildlife and ocean sustainability. What responsibilities and roles have these organizations chosen to focus on in their work?
4. A number of nonprofit and government organizations working with wildlife and ocean conservation have similar or overlapping missions and goals. How should these overlaps be managed? What are the implications for organizational resources and the long-term viability of individual agencies?

5. Common Pool Resources — How do PA's handle the challenges inherent in managing Common pool resources with expansive borders that don't stop inside your area of management or concern?

10

Energy and
Global Climate Change

The world is not running out of energy, but it may be running out of time in making a transition away from the use of fossil fuels. The consumption of fossil fuels emits carbon dioxide and other greenhouse gases, creating changes in temperature and rainfall across the world. The resulting changes, which influence the weather differently in various regions, are collectively referred to as global climate change. In addition, the production of energy based on fossil fuel may be getting more difficult and expensive as global quantities of the resource diminish. Public and private organizations are working to create alternative solutions for sustainable energy management into the future. This chapter discusses the role of public administration in developing sustainable energy infrastructures with reduced negative consequences for the environment. The chapter also will introduce the concepts of peak oil, global climate change, renewable resources, and nuclear energy.

Fossil Fuels and Peak Oil

Peak theory or peak oil is an oil production model designed by M. King Hubbert in the 1950s. The model suggests that oil production will follow a curvilinear trajectory, with a peak in production, after which easy-to-obtain oil diminishes, the cost of production rises significantly, and output is reduced (Heinberg 2000). If the model is explanatory of the amount of oil resources available for production, then dependence on oil for energy is not only un-sustainable in the long run, but also problematic in the near future. A debate has ensued over when peak oil may occur and whether other types of fossil fuel reserves can fill the gap. Hubbert initially suggested that the world would reach peak oil production by the 1970s, although some energy experts say that this deadline may have been extended by high oil prices and reduced consumption during that period. Unfortunately, it is impossible to accurately detect when peak oil may arrive in light of undiscovered reserves and potential technologies. Nevertheless, the world is running out of easy-to-access and low-cost oil, a statement that is hard to refute since oil is a nonrenewable resource (Heinberg 2000).

What are the alternatives to traditional oil production mechanisms for supplying energy? One suggestion is to move toward production of other types of fossil fuels. An example is the development of oil sand production in Alberta, Canada (Chastko 2004). Oil or tar sand is a bituminous soil that is rich in usable petroleum content. In the past, technological limitations and low per-barrel costs of oil prevented its efficient use. As traditional petroleum costs go up, oil sands are becoming a more viable fossil fuel source. The sustainability of oil sand production, however, is questionable. First, oils sand, like all fossil fuels, is nonrenewable. Second, the use of oil for energy, whatever its source, continues to create negative impacts on the environment by contributing to global climate change. Third, oil sand production uses a strip-mining technique, which removes all the top layers of soil and the wildlife they house. The Canadian government requires stripped areas to be replanted to reflect their original form. As mentioned in earlier chapters, however, mature and diverse ecosystems cannot be restored to their original standard very quickly, if at all. The same three barriers exist for coal production and the first two also apply to natural gas production.

Other alternatives to the use of fossil fuel have been recommended. One is the use of other energy sources, such as nuclear energy. Although nuclear power is not a renewable resource using current production measures, it is seen as a potential transition energy resource. Transitional resources are non-renewable and may have some negative environmental consequences, but may serve as all alternative to traditional energy resources as the transformation to renewable energies are made. However, nuclear power is unsustainable in that it produces environmentally damaging radioactive by-products. Renewable resources, such as solar or photovoltaic power, wind or turbine power, wave energy, and geothermal heat, have also been recommended as substitutes for fossil fuels. These resources are lauded because they do not contribute to carbon dioxide emissions and global climate change. Finally, pricing mechanisms may be a market solution to a portion of the oil-for-energy problem. As prices for oil go up, individuals may use less fossil fuel for energy, thereby extending the transition period opportunities further into the future. Price increases also stimulate the production of previously uneconomic alternative resources. Also, firms or governments may create markets for the right to pollute, requiring purchase of the right to emit carbon dioxide into the atmosphere. The amount of emissions should go down if the price of the carbon credits is high enough. A number of these solutions will be discussed in greater detail in the following sections of this chapter.

Buying the Right to Pollute

Al Gore's 2006 movie, *An Inconvenient Truth*, caught the attention of citizens around the world. The film outlined the link between global climate change and carbon dioxide emissions across the world. The film received an Academy Award for best documentary, and Al Gore shared the 2007 Nobel Peace Prize with the Intergovernmental Panel on Climate Change. Since then, global climate change has become a household word.

A number of organizations have since made commitments to reduce their carbon dioxide emissions. Universities across the United States, for instance, have signed onto the American College and University Presidents Climate Commitment, an initiative led by college presidents to reduce emissions from buildings, vehicles, appliances, heating and cooling systems, and other sources. One suggested method of addressing carbon emissions is the purchasing of carbon credits. A carbon credit is the value of a net reduction in carbon dioxide emissions. Organizations or nations may sell or trade carbon credits to organizations or nations whose output of emissions exceeds those set by treaty or regulations. Some non-profit organizations use a variety of mechanisms to remove carbon dioxide from the atmosphere—for instance, by maintaining a large amount of green space or by producing renewable energy resources in excess of their needs. Other organizations may then purchase these credits to offset their own high rate of emissions. Carbon offsets are practices by organizations that correct for their carbon dioxide emissions into the environment. As described in Chapter 2, a market has emerged for exchanging carbon credits in order to offset carbon emissions.

The 1997 Kyoto Protocol is an international agreement wherein more than 180 parties have committed to reducing the greenhouse gases carbon dioxide, methane, nitrous oxide, hydrofluorocarbons, perfluorocarbons, and sulfur hexafluoride. Developed countries signing onto the agreement must make the most significant cuts to emissions relative to undeveloped countries. The United States has not signed the treaty, arguing that developed nations are being asked to bear too much of the burden of reducing greenhouse gas emissions. Developed countries may face enormous economic costs if their manufacturing and transportation systems must cease some of their production in order to meet the Kyoto limits. Supporters of the agreement argue that developed countries should bear a larger burden because they are responsible for a larger portion of total global emissions. An emerging solution to this problem in the European Union is the trading of carbon credits. Less developed countries that produce emissions below their Kyoto limits would sell their credits to developed nations with deficits.

Market-based solutions such as trading carbon credits are seen as a potential means of reducing overall climate emissions due to greenhouse gas emissions. In essence, property rights are assigned to pollution. The redistribution of wealth in carbon trading makes this option controversial. Specifically, poor and underdeveloped nations have the ability to trade their carbon credits for monetary gains, but must at the same time agree to limit any development that might increase their carbon dioxide emissions into the future. This hinders development in these countries and allows developed countries to continue to emit at their current levels, as long as they purchase carbon credits. In particular, the distribution of the initial allowances to emit pollutants is a challenging economic and political issue. The initial amount of pollutants that can be emitted by a nation is determined by treaty or agreement in this model of carbon credit trading. The problem is that the amount of emissions is politically influence and not based solely on scientific knowledge. Consequences include that the total output of carbon dioxide emissions by all nations may still be too high for sustainability, that not all parties may agree to the terms of the treaties, that the process may limit underdeveloped countries in their economic growth, and that the selling of carbon credits may not serve as a catalyst for wealthy countries to alter their behaviors in the long-run, as long as they can afford the purchase of offsets.

Policies, Incentives, and Renewable Energy Resources

Public and nonprofit organizations have a major role in sustainable development in the field of energy. Sustainable development can provide planning for transition from fossil fuel resources to renewable resources and can guide infrastructure development for growth of renewable energy production. Examples of transition-related interventions include the following:

- *Support for energy efficient and environmentally friendly products.* The U.S. government's Energy Star program provides citizens with information about appliances that consume low amounts of energy, for instance.
- *Incentives for improving residential and business energy efficiency.* An example is Great Britain's provision of free home insulation to residents who are more than 70 years old and those with low income-related benefits.

- *Support for mass transit, carpooling, and other low-energy transportation systems.* A number of organizations are promoting car-free local communities in order to reduce energy use and emissions.
- *Education on short-term solutions.* A number of nonprofit and public organizations provide information on how to reduce energy consumption.

In addition to these transitional supports, nonprofit and public agencies can support larger infrastructural changes to create sustainable energy systems. To achieve consumption-related changes, agencies can try to modify human behavior through education and incentives in order to encourage lifestyles that are more sustainable. For instance, encouraging citizens to buy energy-efficient vehicles and purchase homes in densely populated environments rather than in suburban ones should lead to reduced energy consumption in vehicles. Citizens' lifestyle changes must be supported by viable alternatives in order to be effective. If citizens are encouraged to drive less, for instance, then alternatives using less energy, such as mass transit, must be available to them.

Governments and nonprofit organizations can also support the development of renewable energy production and infrastructure. Because most renewable energy technologies may perform well in some environments but not in others, no one form of renewable energy may be a perfect substitute for fossil fuel. For instance, some communities may have ideal average wind speed for the installation of wind turbines, while others have to high or too low of wind speeds. In another example, solar or photovoltaic energy may be most viable in regions with a high number of sunny days. This suggests that nonprofit and public organizations can be a critical resource for development, research, and education in the field. As the cost of development will be high due to the number of technologies involved and their success in contextualized settings, public administration may be able to fill some of the gaps in knowledge, funding, education, and infrastructure.

A number of renewable energies are currently in the spotlight. Several of them are described below:

- *Solar or photovoltaic energy* (energy derived from harnessing heat and light energy from the sun). This technology is most effective in regions with consistent levels of sunlight. The energy can be transferred to electricity for general use. Alternative energy sources may be required as backup in seasons with low levels of sunlight. The high cost of installation and materials can be prohibitive for some citizens.
- *Wind or turbine power* (energy derived from wind). Wind turbines have been used for centuries to power mills and to pump water. Wind power

can also be transferred to electricity for general use. Systems require steady winds and have been criticized because of their aesthetics, noise, and the potential danger to migrating and breeding birds.

- *Wave energy* (energy harnessed from the rocking motion of ocean waves). The energy can be transferred to electricity.
- *Geothermal energy* (heat energy from Earth's core). The heat can be directly applied to heat water and buildings and to turn turbines. It can be used to create electricity.
- *Hydrogen and fuel cell technologies* (a developing set of technologies using hydrogen delivery and storage). Replacement of combustion engines in automobiles is a major objective of fuel cell development.
- *Hydropower or hydroelectric power* (energy from artificial and natural water systems). A number of dams, with 2,338 hyrodoelectric plants in the United States, generate to create electricity, and 28 million households in the United States use hydropower (Hall and Reeves 2006; U.S. Department of Energy 2008).

It is possible that a number of these energy technologies and others will develop under standard free-market systems. Many for-profit organizations have started investing in development of these technologies. Support from public and nonprofit agencies in the forms of policy development and advocacy, funding and resource provision, education and research, and planning would speed the transition. Further, governments and nonprofits may have an even more important role in coordinating multiple technologies and infrastructures since no one of the alternative technologies is likely to be a perfect replacement for fossil fuel.

Questions to Consider

1. Are carbon credit purchases a reasonable worldwide solution for reducing carbon dioxide emissions?
2. Should developed nations have a higher degree of responsibility for developing alternative energy resources and addressing global climate change than less developed countries?
3. Global climate change has received a great deal of political attention in the United States in recent years. Has this attention had a positive impact on managing human influences on global climate change?

11

Higher Education

One of the most important contributors to environmental sustainable development may be colleges, their faculty, their students, and their community stakeholders. Not only is sustainable development often a part of the college curriculum, but institutional research and community service can transform communities by increasing knowledge about natural capital. Public institutions of higher learning, as public agencies, have a responsibility to translate knowledge to citizens and to disseminate information for community impact. This chapter reviews how colleges can catalyze community environmental sustainability and how public administrators can partner with institutions of higher learning to build strong sustainable development plans. Through community service, curriculum-building, and college construction and maintenance, colleges can be a critical force in sustainable development.

To begin, colleges have one very important asset that can be tied directly to sustainable development: they are the caretakers of environmental knowledge held within a number of disciplines. This means that faculty members in the departments of the social and natural sciences can take part in research and curriculum development that can advance sustainable development practice in the community. Since sustainable development requires system thinking, interdisciplinary exchange and knowledge-building may be the most important asset offered by colleges to address environmental problems. Because many of the environmental problems addressed by sustainability planning are complex, requiring a number of areas of decision-making expertise, institutions of higher learning can be a resource for research, assessment, information-gathering, and training. In addition, students may contribute to the community as interns, through service learning, and through classroom research projects.

Colleges also have the opportunity to act as an experimental site for much

Exhibit 11.1　**College Environmental System Components**

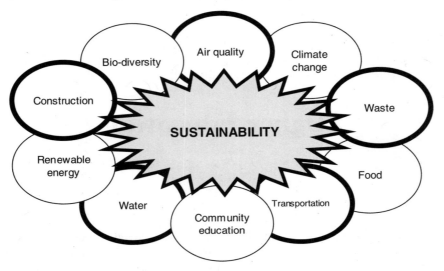

of the research that is required for sustainable development. Exhibit 11.1 shows the types of system components that are managed daily in the physical plant of the college. Green building and renovation, recycling programs, carbon footprint reduction, renewable energy use, and the use of organic foods in cafeterias are examples of the transformations taking place today. Hundreds of colleges and universities across the United States have signed onto the Presidents Climate Commitment Task Force, an initiative led by college presidents to integrate climate neutrality and sustainable practices into teaching, research, and outreach. As early as 2001, many institutions, such as Tufts, St. Lawrence University, and the University of Georgia, had already adopted broad environmental policy statements (Creighton 2001). The number of universities committing to such policies continues to expand. Colleges, as they rebuild their own institutions based on sustainable practices, can provide information about their lessons learned to the community. The work of colleges internally and with their communities can inform many decisions that could benefit human beings and their environments.

Because of the number and types of goods and services they provide under a usually centralized decision-making process, institutions of higher learning can be ideal places to practice system component changes. For faculty and students traveling to the campus site, the college can consider various transportation systems. For instance, colleges can test the impact of free or paid parking on automobile use on campus. Colleges can also implement

The Morrow Plots at the University of Illinois

Many American universities were chartered specifically to demonstrate and disseminate improvements in agricultural and industrial practices. One historic and visible illustration is the Morrow Plots at the University of Illinois at Urbana-Champaign—a National Historic Landmark consisting of three plots covering less than an acre near the center of campus. Established in 1876, they stand as the oldest agronomic experimental plot in the United States; one of them is the oldest continuously planted corn plot in the world. Their purpose is to be a working laboratory for experiments with fertilizer and crop rotation to determine their effect on corn yields. The original founders of the Morrow Plots, Professors George Morrow and Manley Miles, asked the same questions that arise today in discussions of sustainability: "If corn were grown year after year on the same field, would yields decline? How soon would this decline come and how severe would it be? If corn were alternated or rotated with other crops, would that help to maintain the soil's productivity?" The use of campus facilities and the experimental method suggests a way to test theories of sustainability today.

Source: Crop Sciences Research and Education Center, University of Illinois at Urbana-Champaign, "The Morrow Plots: A Century of Learning." www.cropsci.uiuc.edu/research/rdc/urbana/morrow.cfm.

a number of public transportation options and assess the impacts of each option individually or in combinations with other options. Further, college dorms and administrative buildings allow for improvement of construction, water, waste, and energy components. Various designs and approaches can be tested on campuses and applied to both residential and administrative building construction in other settings. Also, the cafeteria can experiment with the provision of organic and locally grown foods and reduce the use of nonenvironmentally friendly production materials such as plastic wraps and Styrofoam contrainers. By testing the viability of such practices within a small, easily controlled system, colleges are enabled to make recommendations for larger community settings.

Colleges also have the opportunity to partner with other colleges and with their local community to implement large-scale structural changes. Partnering with other institutions can reduce some of the costs of research and information-gathering for project development. Further, stakeholders in this larger plan can learn from other stakeholder action in order to improve subsequent plans and designs. This chapter will begin by talking about physical infrastructure improvements promoted by colleges and then discuss the role of curriculum change related to environmental sustainability. It will discuss how public administrators can actively partner with institutions of higher learning to meet environmental sustainability goals.

Constructing an Environmentally Friendly College Community

In 2006, seventeen U.S. states required or promoted green building practices in public construction (Massachusetts Sustainable Design Roundtable 2006). One of the leading certification programs for green construction is the Leadership in Energy and Environmental Design (LEED) Green Building Rating System developed by the U.S. Green Building Council. It provides guidelines for green construction, maintenance, and design of buildings in the United States. Other popular assessment and certification tools are Comprehensive Assessment Systems for Building Environmental Efficiency (CASBEE) in Japan, Building Research Establishment Environmental Assessment Method (BREEAM) in the United Kingdom, Green Star, Sustainable Development Assessment Tool, and the green building tool titled GBtool. All these tools attempt to assess various components of the construction system and to provide a standardized approach to meeting sustainability goals. The application of these methods allows users to compare building site to building site. The tools also provide a baseline for measuring sustainable practices.

LEED establishes public construction standards for sustainable sites, water efficiency, energy and atmosphere, materials and resources, indoor environmental quality, and innovation and design process (Kats and Capital E 2006). A "deep understanding of natural systems," of human-centered values, and of long-term consequences is required (Childs and Croxton 2005). CASBEE focuses on energy and resource efficiency and on local and indoor environments. BREEAM addresses energy efficiency, carbon dioxide emissions, water efficiency, surface water management, waste management, and use of materials. These assessment tools allow colleges and other institutions investing in construction projects to improve resource use in their physical infrastructure and maintenance.

Although these certification tools are a helpful starting place for any organization interested in environmental sustainability, their weakness is that they offer tradeoffs in order to meet a minimum level of guidelines. Many tools use point systems that allow an organization to choose the lowest cost changes and improvements as long as it earns the minimum number of points. This means that, as long as they receive their certification, organizations may refrain from tackling the most meaningful investments whose economic cost is high in the short run. Holistic approaches to effective environmental change may be more beneficial and often less costly in the long run, but they may also be a hard sell to decision-makers if the initial costs are high.

As all organizations have limited financial resources, with often even tighter budgets for public and nonprofit agencies, they must often make tradeoffs. For instance, a college may purchase new, energy-efficient washers and dryers for dormitory buildings, but refrain from replacing existing machines until they wear out. Institutions may choose Silver LEED certification standards instead of Gold LEED standards, which are more rigorous and more costly to achieve. The dialogue over tradeoffs and budget constraints has costs itself. The initial costs of environmentally sustainable construction design are high. When plans are altered during the construction process because of budget limits, there are the additional costs of the design change as well as the long-run costs of not using the most efficient processes. Flexible planning, however, is necessary when the technologies are new, prices may change, and budgets may be reduced. Colleges absorb some of the costs of uncertainty when they are front-runners in the use of new green technologies. However, their research and experimentation can reduce the cost of building for other public and nonprofit institutions. Exhibit 11.2 offers examples of possible physical infrastructure improvements available to institutions of higher learning.

When considering the potential contribution of college construction projects to sustainable development knowledge-building, it is important to discuss not only the building of new structures, but also the renovation of existing ones. The contractual agreements, the physical characteristics of existing structures, and the policies in use in any community setting restrict the extent to which renovation or new construction is possible. The retrofitting of new technologies is often more difficult and costly than their inclusion in new construction. An analysis of the costs and benefits of renovations, including the positive externalities for the community, is a necessity. Raising funds for sustainable construction projects can be challenging, but institutions can initiate a number of other programs that have lesser start-up costs. These lessons, too, can be translated into use by public and nonprofit organizations.

Preparing Students for Civic Responsibility

Management of natural resources in light of growth is an important problem for students and faculty at institutions of higher learning, on a personal scale, at an institutional scale, at a local scale, and at the international scale. Global climate change, air pollution, diminishing fossil fuel resources, and access to clean water are becoming an important part of the dialogue within the college curriculum. An advantage of institutions of higher learning is their unique

Exhibit 11.2

Sustainability Improvements in Higher Education Construction

Resource category	Planning applications to improve sustainability
Construction, energy, and land management	Choosing sustainable construction using renewable, readily available materials (e.g., concrete, recycled materials, straw build, mud build)
	Using materials indigenous or local to the community
	Remodeling to improve energy efficiency and fit with new technologies
	Repairing and reconstructing failing infrastructural components (e.g., leaking underground water or steam pipes or single-walled fuel storage units)
	Using materials with low environmental impact in case the building's materials become waste when the building is destroyed or reconstructed
	Using high-efficiency insulation with low environmental impact
	Creating energy-efficient envelopes for heat management, possibly including passive solar energy
	Using renewable energy systems with low environmental impact (e.g., solar or wind energy)
	Incorporating natural lighting
	Incorporating recreational outdoor space
	Managing air quality (e.g., filtering and reducing carbon dioxide emissions)
	Using energy-efficient air heating, cooling, and distribution
	Creating and preserving outdoor habitat for native wildlife

Water	Using gray water or using the same water for more than one purpose without purification, for instance to do laundry and then to flush toilets or water lawns with
	Reducing waste water (especially in toilets)
	Conserving drinking water by not using it in processes that do not require purified water, such as using it to water lawns or wash cars
	Using sustainable appliances (e.g., air conditioning, dishwashers, washers and dryers)
Waste	Properly disposing of biohazard waste
	Using waste removal systems with low environmental impact
	Recycling plastics, paper, and glass with individual user incentives and collection areas
	Recycling and managing technology-related waste (e.g., cell phones, computers, automobile oil and fluids)
	Using biodegradable cleaning materials
	Giving special attention to by-products of research (e.g., from chemistry and biology labs)
Food	Educating citizens on food quality and nutrition
	Precycling and recycling food-related packaging
	Incorporating community gardening and strategic landscaping
Transportation	Encouraging use of mass transit systems as an alternative to automobile travel
	Minimizing the amount of space allotted to parking
	Creating biking and walking paths as an alternative to fossil fuel–dependent transportation

109

ability to exist within their local and global environments. Students and faculty, because of their course-related travel and research, have the opportunity to translate knowledge learned in local settings as far apart as Las Vegas and Dubai into information that can be applied to practice. Institutions of higher learning can translate important lessons learned in development across the world into meaningful action in local settings and also report local lessons back out to the world.

The combination of theory and practice in the curriculum, especially in departments or schools of public administration and other community-engaged units, can be an important benefit offered by institutions of higher learning to their communities. Through service learning, students can provide voluntary or paid labor to communities under the direction of experienced faculty members. Students benefit by gaining firsthand experience in planning and decision-making and the community benefits from their knowledge and skills. The use of both applied and theoretical strategies leads to effective sustainable development education for students and to tangible benefits for their communities. Further, real-world experiences, which students tend to perceive as highly relevant for sustainability education, demonstrate community benefits and encourage student responsibility in the delivery of service (Pearson, Honeywood, and O'Toole 2005; Payne 2006). These civic leadership opportunities encourage critical thinking and creative problem resolution in students, allowing them to become better informed and more experienced professionals and more active citizens.

For those institutions of higher learning interested in including sustainability in the curriculum, there are a number of opportunities and challenges. Integration of sustainability into the curriculum can be difficult (Carlson 2006). Conceptual views of teaching and sustainability play a significant role in curriculum development in the public administration or public policy classroom and in professional training programs offered by institutions of higher learning (Reid and Petorz 2006). These conceptions demonstrate the extent to which sustainability has been integrated into the curriculum. For professionals choosing to further their professional education in public administration and public policy programs or for public or nonprofit organizations hiring trainers from colleges to work with their employees, it is important to gauge the extent to which sustainable development is included within curriculum. The curriculum may treat sustainable development as a fully integrated part of a number of subfields such as public sector economics, urban development, and local government administration. It may also consider sustainable development as a separate category that stands on its own. Programs should select curriculum options that best match their organizational culture and goals. Professionals should select training programs that best match their career and subfield goals.

Sustainability in MPA Curricula

The National Association of Schools of Public Affairs and Administration (NASPAA) sets standards for master's programs in public administration (MPA) and public policy (MPP) that seek to be accredited. Among those standards are the competencies expected of all MPA and MPP graduates. New standards go into effect in the fall of 2009. Standard 1.1 applies to the mission statement of all accredited MPA and MPP programs. As of this writing, the proposed standard lists three required elements of the mission statement, one of which requires the program to articulate "its purpose and core values such as ethics, fiscal and environmental sustainability, and social equity given the program's particular emphasis on public affairs, administration, and policy."

Source: NASPAA Standards Review 2009: Proposed Accreditation Standards, February 20, 2009. www.naspaa.org/accreditation/standard2009/docs/Standards2009Draft2.20.09. pdf

Public administration and public policy programs can use various methods to incorporate sustainable development into the curriculum. The selection of specific inclusion options depends upon the subject matter of a course and upon the vision of the program in which it is housed. The use of different options within the department curriculum can offer faculty and students the opportunity to develop and translate knowledge that is useful for various community stakeholders (Exhibit 11.3).

In addition to inclusion within a formal college curriculum, sustainable development education also can benefit community agencies and their employees. In selecting training programs or trainers, it is important for an agency to communicate the desired outcomes to the training team. Facilitating a sustainable development plan, although it often includes education of an agency's employees and administrators, is a very different process from purely educational sessions that are not meant to lead to direct, immediate action. Many organizations offer training sessions to their employees to stimulate discussion and professional development. Other organizations offer training that is intended to lead to immediate, practical results. Training may be focused on process, assessment, planning, and/or outcomes. For instance, an agency that intends to build an environmentally sustainable building might benefit from discussions with a public administration expert about planning, cost-benefit analysis, and decision-making; an architect who is knowledgeable in sustainable design implementation; a professional trained to facilitate

Exhibit 11.3

Incorporating Environmental Sustainability Into the Classroom

Options	Description
Case studies	The course includes specific cases or applications of sustainable development: for example, specific changes in environmental policy, examples of innovations, or specific examples of agency action. (Chase 1998)
Single-topic sustainability course	The course focuses entirely on the topic of sustainable development or includes specific units dedicated to the topic within the course. (Chase 1998)
Research projects	Students complete sustainability-related research for course credit or as part of independent study.
Service learning	Under the guidance of the instructor, students undertake projects focusing on sustainability issues in the community. Community nonprofits and leaders are included in the design of the service-learning project.
Guest experts	Expert professionals from the community are invited to present current issues in sustainable development.
Conference presentation	Students participate in sustainability-focused conferences for credit, presenting their own research as appropriate.
Mission change	The department commits itself to integrating sustainability into the curriculum. Critical educational objectives are met by collaboration between instructors. (Chase 1998)
Small group discussion	Students are encouraged to research and discuss specific sustainability issues within the classroom. (Chase 1998)
Interdisciplinary courses	Interdisciplinary courses are designed in coordination with other departments. Guest instructors from other disciplines may be invited into the public administration classroom to enhance the curriculum. (Bosselman 2001)
Distance education	Students use distance-mediated education tools for international and multiregional collaboration on sustainability issues.
Applied research	Faculty members, perhaps with the assistance of students, complete research for community partners.

LEED-certified design; and members of other organizations that have already completed similar projects.

Clarity of organizational and individual vision, as public administrators approach their training and education in sustainable development, can have an impact on the success of planning, action, and outcomes. There may be no single best approach, but the best approaches should align with the goals of the individual and the organization.

Providing Research Data for Community Use

As mentioned earlier, institutions of higher learning provide research that is critical for public projects development. Data- and research-driven decision-making in communities is a vital part of effective sustainable development. Colleges reduce transaction costs of sustainable development projects by acting as warehouses of information, by providing faculty and student labor and expertise in information-gathering, by serving as models for technological development, and by providing interdisciplinary exchange on important environmental issues. When institutions make information public, then the costs of information-gathering for citizens and private stakeholders are reduced. Research is a positive externality of higher education; public subsidies of research encourage increased research. These college research projects can reduce the cost of development in the long run and therefore encourage sustainable development. Public administration programs can also provide training in strategic planning, cost-benefit analysis, and assessment to enhance community capacity for sustainable development. The relationships built between the college and the community can build social capital, encouraging sustainable development.

Sharing information with communities may be one of the most important roles of institutions of higher learning. Creating public records of information gathered through institutional research projects is most effective when it is translated for use by several types of users. Information may be formatted so that it is suitable for citizens, for expert professionals, and for other researchers specializing in the field. Summaries of information can be the starting place for citizens who are beginning their exploration of environmental issues. Additional data and technical information can be made available for more expert citizens and professionals. Transaction costs are further reduced when citizens and professionals have the ability to directly find the information they need. Colleges are increasingly providing online resources to transmit information relevant to specific populations and regions. Tools such as geographic information systems (GIS) can provide demographic and geographic data to enhance decision-making.

CHAPTER 11

The Role of Public Administration

As is clear by now, no discipline has a monopoly on the topic of sustainability. The natural sciences identified and defined it. Public administration has its own relevance to sustainability. Public administration is crucial to this issue because of its integrative capacity. It is a field of study that brings together all other disciplines that are relevant to understanding and implementing policy. Understanding the problems of sustainability requires some knowledge of science; understanding solutions for sustainability requires some knowledge of public administration. Ultimately, steps to address unsustainable practice need to be implemented by public and nonprofit (and for-profit) organizations. Agencies need to be given authority, money, and staff. Managing all these resources requires knowledge of public administration. When public administrators do their job right, they can help society achieve effective, efficient, and equitable solutions. Whether sustainable development is a part of the teaching, research, or service mission of a college, educational institutions of all kinds can be venues for discovery and demonstration of sustainable practice.

Questions to Consider

1. How can information on sustainable development be disseminated in a manner that is useful for a variety of community stakeholder groups?
2. A number of organizations set minimum certification standards for green construction projects. How are LEED and other certification standards meaningful and effective means of assessing and encouraging environmentally sustainable construction?
3. How is sustainability included in the NASPAA standards for MPA and MPP programs? If you are in an MPA or MPP program (or considering one), how does your program cover the topic in the mission statement of the program? How could your program improve its attempts to educate MPA and MPP students about sustainability?

12

Measurement and Assessment

Once organizations have made the commitment to invest in sustainable development planning and practice, how do they know they are meeting their goals successfully? Selecting the appropriate tools to assess the meaningful implementation of sustainable development can be difficult. As discussed in earlier chapters, the first step is to integrate assessment fully into the decision-making process, at initial development stages and at regular intervals thereafter. Many sustainability-related assessment tools are undertaken outside of the large organizational plan, reducing their effectiveness. Second, measurement of outcomes as well as outputs is a key consideration. It is important for organizations to clarify the goals they want to achieve before investing in action steps. Especially because many desired outcomes are not easily quantifiable, the assessment team must clarify and define goals and objectives. Finally, the large number of assessment and decision-making tools available to public administrators makes assessment and measurement difficult. Administrators need to identify which of the many types of tools is best adapted to inform decision-making in their organization.

Strong outcomes rely on a good match between organizational goals and assessment tools. There is no single tool that meets the needs of all organizations and each of their specific sustainability goals. One organization may use a number of tools in the decision-making process, while another may use only one tool for a project with a limited scope. Also, the organization may need to adapt existing tools to meet its own needs. This chapter will discuss types of sustainable development measurement tools, goal and objective setting, and assessment integration. It also will offer recommendations for selection of assessment tools that meet organizational needs.

Balancing Inputs, Outputs, and Outcomes

Chapter 1 of this book discussed the relationship between inputs, outputs, and outcomes. Effective decision-making on the part of any organization requires the documentation of all three. Leaders should know what resources they have invested, what has been produced as a result, and what impacts have resulted. Whenever public and nonprofit organizations invest in projects and programs, whether directly related to sustainable development or not, there is an opportunity to include sustainability in the decision-making process. The first step in any decision-making process, therefore, is to commit to a formal plan of action that documents resource expenditures and objective and subjective indicators of success. The plan, whether it is a strategic plan or another type of planning process, allows the stakeholders in the decision-making process to translate goals into action. The process of planning itself translates and prioritizes knowledge and information held by stakeholders, and in many cases improves buy-in, transparency, and citizen inclusion.

A common type of planning used in public administration is strategic planning. Strategic planning ties resources to the agency's mission and vision, establishes goals and objectives for the organization and its stakeholders, sets timelines for projects, identifies evaluation methods, and establishes responsibility for tasks. The planning process includes in the decision-making process stakeholders with various interests in the organizational outcomes and also ensures that the organization takes its strengths and weaknesses into consideration. The most important steps in implementing strategic planning are the following:

- A decision by organizational leaders to complete a strategic plan
- Establishing the parameters of the plan, or whether the plan will be applied to the entire organization or to subunits
- Allocation of resources for strategic planning by the leadership
- Recruitment and selection of project facilitators and lead organizational managers responsible for planning
- Selection of citizens and organizational stakeholders to be involved in the planning process
- Consideration and possible revision of the organizational vision and mission
- Consideration of the internal strength and weakness of the organization (the S and W of SWOT analysis), including analysis of data regarding employees, citizens or service recipients, and finances and the possible collection of new data
- Consideration of the external opportunities and threats for the organiza-

Exhibit 12.1   **Sample Section of a Strategic Planning Document**

GOAL ONE:					
Objective	Tasks	Resources	Responsible parties	Task start and completion dates	Evaluation method and period
1.	a. b. c.				
2.	a. b. c.				

tion (the O and T of SWOT analysis), including analysis of competition, demographic changes in the community population, and changes in community service needs
- Review of the issues that could be potential projects for the organization and discussion of the community problems it may want to solve
- Setting priorities for potential projects based on match with the organizational mission and vision, available resources, and legal and regulatory limits
- Identification of related goals and objectives
- Assignment of tasks to objectives
- Assignment of resources, responsible parties, and timelines to tasks
- Assignment of assessment methods to goals, objectives, and tasks

The above steps only partially explain how a strategic plan can be implemented by an organization. The assistance of an expert facilitator and training for key organizational plan leaders can be critical to its success. The value of the planning process is only as strong as the expertise of the project leaders and the depth of commitment of all stakeholders to the action and decision steps. Strategic planning can be a strong decision-making tool if it is implemented with rigor and care. It also has the potential to be tied to sustainable development planning because it already considers resource use in the plan.

Exhibit 12.1 demonstrates how goals and objectives in a strategic planning document may be organized. The organization has the opportunity to consider sustainable development each time a resource enters into the plan.

Each section in Exhibit 12.1 represents a segment of the planning process and all require ongoing assessment and adaptation as the organization changes. The sections and their purpose are defined below:

- *Goal.* A goal states a specific desired outcome. It should be tied directly to the mission and vision of the organization.
- *Objective.* An objective breaks down the goal into smaller steps and often is stated in terms of outputs. These outputs often serve as indicators of the success of the outcome.
- *Tasks.* Tasks are specific actions taken in order to achieve the objective. They often are placed in chronological order in the plan.
- *Resources.* Resources are the capital, labor, and time resources needed to achieve goals and objectives. They often are tied to specific objectives and are allocated by the leadership of the organization. The resource step is an opportunity to consider alternative means of achieving the task, taking into account efficiency and environmental sustainability.
- *Responsible parties.* Responsible parties are assigned to all tasks. Tasks may be defined in terms of individual positions or may be assigned to committees or groups of individuals.
- *Task start and completion dates.* Dates for beginning and finishing each task are assigned.
- *Evaluation method and period.* The tools used for assessment and the frequency of their use also are included.

In any plan put forth by an organization, setting measurable goals and objectives is vital. The establishment of goals and objectives prior to action allows organizations to focus their resources on outcomes and outputs. Indicators of success are coordinated with the action steps or tasks.

Types of Assessment

There are hundreds of environmental sustainability assessment tools available to organizations. A number of popular tools have been used to standardize measurement, and many organizations invent and modify assessment tools to meet their own need. When identifying which tools to use for assessment of sustainability in an organization, administrators need to consider the various types of measurement possible. Some of these possibilities are discussed in the following paragraphs and also are described in Exhibit 12.2.

First, public administrators have the option to consider what impact phase to focus on. Impact phases can be process-, product-, or results-oriented. Is the public administrator more interested in the steps taken toward decision-making or in the results? Assessment tools can explore the process by which sustainable action is undertaken. Are the action and the decision-making steps the most effective ones for achieving sustainability? These tools help organizations understand how internal planning and action structures influence goal achieve-

Exhibit 12.2 **Potential Types of Assessment**

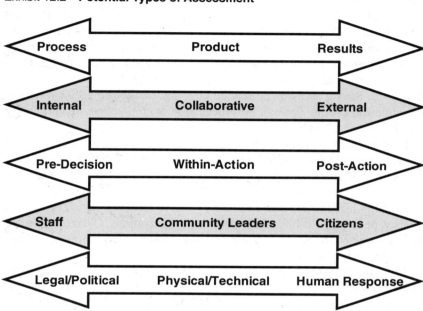

Process	Product	Results
Internal	Collaborative	External
Pre-Decision	Within-Action	Post-Action
Staff	Community Leaders	Citizens
Legal/Political	Physical/Technical	Human Response

ment. The tools can also consider output measures, which assess the quality and quantity of the product. These tools also help organizations determine the efficiency and effectiveness of their methods of transforming resources into outputs. Assessment tools also can determine the success of outcomes, or the match between intended and actual results of action. Organizations also can determine if goals and outcomes are properly aligned. Often, it makes sense to evaluate process, product, and results at various stages of planning.

Second, administrators decide where they want to measure the scope of the assessment. Are they interested in exploring the organization itself or the community in which it is immersed? Internal measures involve the assessment of the organization's own successes. For example, the organization may research the impact of its actions on its own carbon footprint. External measures assess the aggregate impact of the organization's actions on the community or on society. The scope of the assessment also may be focused on the collaborative actions of systems of organizations in which the original organization is just one part. The scope, in this instance, is neither wholly internal nor external to the organization, but rather explores the impacts of shared action and planning.

Third, the timing of the assessment also is important to consider. Timing addresses the period in which research is undertaken as well as its frequency. Predecision evaluation, used to guide planning, assesses research undertaken prior to action. Within-action evaluation takes place during the action, and postaction, performance-based evaluation occurs after action is completed. This last type of evaluation considers the impact of action after implementation of all or part of the plan. Evaluation may be undertaken at all of the periods described. Strong assessment may be ongoing, tied to the decision-making schedule and cycling through the predecision, within-action, and postaction phases on a regular basis.

Fourth, evaluation must consider whose actions will be evaluated. Which stakeholders will the assessment focus on? For instance, assessment could focus on staff members internal to the organization: managers, the employees they supervise, and agency volunteers. Or the assessment could focus on community leaders, political and administrative leaders working outside the agency, perhaps including leaders of other organizations. Citizen action also can be assessed, focusing on the behavior of community members with ties to the organization.

Fifth, the tools available to assess sustainability also can address a variety of structures. Assessment may explore legal and political structures, including the policies, regulations, and laws potentially impacting agency decisions. Assessment tools also may consider physical and technical factors, such as buildings and associated systems. Technological alternatives and advances related to physical structures may also be considered. Finally, human response structures may also be evaluated. This type of assessment considers how people respond to other types of structures.

The number of decision-making dimensions that may require assessment in sustainable development measurement may seem overwhelming. Organizations across the world are working to translate measurement tools into working, applicable, meaningful, and holistic devices. A number of assessment tools that have been created for use by practitioners will be discussed in the coming paragraphs, along with their specific strengths in application. In the end, each organization needs to do what works best for its stakeholders. Commitment to following the process is often more important than picking the right process. This is because planning, decision making, and assessment tools may be modified and improved to match the specific needs and characteristics of each organization.

Cost-Benefit Analysis

As discussed in Chapter 2, cost-benefit analysis (CBA) is a systematic process for comparing the costs of a project to the benefits in order to evaluate

---

Discounting Formula for Costs and Benefits

Calculating the present value (PV) of receiving a future value (FV) of $100 two years into the future requires the use of the formula for discounting. Discounting is the logical opposite of compounded interest. The formula for discounting is

$$PV = FV/(1 + r)^n,$$

where r is the discount rate and n is the number of years into the future that the future value is received. In this example, FV is $100, n is 2, and we assume a value for r of 3 percent. Plugging these values into the formula gives

$$PV = \$100/1.0609 = \$94.26.$$

The higher the discount rate and the longer the period of time, the smaller PV is relative to FV.

---

its efficiency. A project is accepted if its net benefits (benefits minus costs) are greater than zero. Another way to calculate the CBA is to calculate the ratio of benefits divided by costs, accepting projects whose ratio is greater than one.

Accurate calculation of the costs and benefits is therefore critically important. All expenses should be included: purchases, intangible costs such as the cost of pollution, and opportunity costs such as the value of unvalued resources used in the project (donated labor or land are common examples). Benefits are usually more difficult to calculate than costs because there may be no market for some goods, such as prevention programs that demonstrate difficult to quantify benefits in the short-run, but that might have significant benefits on health or well being in the long run. Despite this challenge, several clever ways to calculate the value of nonmarketed goods have been devised. For instance, values have been estimated for reducing noise pollution near airports by examining the impact of noise on housing values; national parks can be valued by determining how much people paid to travel to visit them. Often ranges of values can be estimated to recognize the difficulty of establishing an exact value.

Comparing costs and benefits realized at different times requires using the process of discounting values. This recognizes that a dollar received today is worth more than a dollar received in five years because the funds could be put to use in this period of time by investing them. The process of discounting converts all future values into current values, which then can be mathematically manipulated. See the box on page 121 for the discounting formula and an example.

Once costs and benefits are accurately determined and converted into present values, the calculations of net benefits and the cost-benefit ratio are easy. The results allow for comparison of the efficiency of a wide variety of projects. One common approach is to calculate the cost-to-benefit ratio of several programs, rank them by the ratio from high to low, and then do the highest-valued projects first, moving down the list until funds are exhausted. This method allows for the efficient selection of competing projects.

Buildings and Construction

One of the most costly investments an organization makes is in the construction of its buildings. Funders are interested in the reduction of short-term costs. Because green building increases the costs of construction by an average of 2 percent, it is important to consider the returns on this investment in terms of environmental impact and in terms of costs (Kats and Capital E 2003). If there are to be cost savings in the long run, it is critical that the savings be discussed during the decision-making process. Any savings reducing the magnitude of the initial investment, even if it is not higher than the short-term costs, also is critical to include. One of the most effective tools to address long run and short-run costs is the cost-benefit analysis.

The application of cost-benefit analysis to construction projects can be an arduous process. Insufficient information about technologies and their development, lack of resources to determine life cycle costs, and incomplete integration between and within systems or projects can make cost-benefit analysis difficult (Kats and Capital E 2006). Decision-makers should guide the analysis by considering a number of critical information sources, including project manuals, green feasibility studies, cost estimates of construction, architectural design documents, energy modeling reports, and project budgets (HMFH Architects and Vermont Energy Investment Corp. 2005). Access to many of these reports often requires the assistance of planning, engineering, and construction professionals. Information is not necessarily accessible to persons acting as decision-makers in organizations and may require consultation with technical experts.

Finally, the establishment of a time horizon for assessment purposes is itself difficult. Common assessment periods include five years, twenty-five years, and one hundred years after construction is completed. The time horizon should take into account when and if the building will eventually recoup the

Exhibit 12.3   **Sample Aggregation Chart for Cost-Benefit Analysis**

	Benefit	Cost	Net cost or benefit per category	Total cost or benefit
Electricity				
Construction materials				
Waste				
Heating and cooling equipment				
Appliances				
Land				
Water				
Research and development				
Permits				
Certifications				
Other				

initial investment in environmentally sustainable construction. It should also project when the building will have to be replaced or significantly remodeled. A cost-benefit model for several time horizons is important. Exhibit 12.3 provides a simple sample version of a cost-benefit decision-making tool for application in sustainable development.

The Value of Rigorous, Established Assessment Tools

Not all benefits and costs can be translated into quantifiable financial data. Meaningful assessment provides both quantitative and qualitative data to direct decision-making. The rigor of the research and the availability of data over long periods of time improve decision-making. Research design and tools must be matched to the type of action and related decision-making of each organization and its projects.

One such excellent tool, for example, is the Famine Early Warning Systems Network (FEWSNET), which provides the type of decision-making power that is both rigorous and critical to planning and plan implementation. This network collects physical and social data that inform relief action in eastern Africa. Researchers collect physical data about rainfall, temperature, and vegetation cover through remote sensing. These data, downloaded from satellites, are used to determine the nature of the growing season in famine-susceptible countries so that emergency response can be organized in time to provide appropriate relief. In most cases, remote-sensing data guide decisions even before the growing season starts, using climate prediction to mobilize assistance that takes up to nine months to reach intended communities. The data, collected using federal funds and made publicly available, allows researchers to track climate change. In the long term, FEWSNET could provide information about the impact of climate change in Africa and across the world.

Famine, of course, is not caused directly by climate variables. How citizens respond to growing seasons, climate, and agricultural change can damage or improve food security. For instance, if a community is able to prepare for future natural crises in agriculture by setting aside surplus goods from a bountiful year, the impact on the community may not be as harsh. If surplus, instead, causes agriculture prices to fall, reducing planting during the following, drought-ridden year, the crisis can be made much worse. Social data about human behavior, therefore, must also inform decision-making.

Using highly rigorous, well-established assessment steps makes it possible for organizations to anticipate future needs and to obtain needed support for action. Another benefit of connecting agency research to existing research is that the organization can continue to build the pool of information needed for long-term success in sustainability decisions. When possible, it is in an organization's best interest to review existing research in the form of published articles and public documents before committing to a research agenda. Collaboration with government agencies and institutions of higher learning can improve the rigor of the research while also adding to the pool of knowledge.

For many types of sustainable development–related research, agencies can use available assessment tools that have been developed and improved over time. The Leadership in Energy and Environmental Design (LEED) Green Building Rating System certification process for construction projects is such an example. These tools can be extremely helpful for organizations just starting to adopt environmentally sustainable practices. The key, however, is to ensure that any tool is customized to the organization and its goals. Rigor and customization of tools such as strategic planning and cost-benefit analysis determine their success. Decisions that are driven by knowledge, information, and data gathered through well-designed research are most likely to achieve desired outcomes. At the same time, tools should be relevant and answer the questions facing an organization without too much time and cost.

Recommendations for Selecting an Assessment Tool

The precise tool that is most effective for organizational assessment of sustainability depends on the desired outcome, the scope of the project, the nature of the project, the availability of resources, the technical rigor required in decision-making, and the expertise of the organization's leaders and facilitators. Because sustainability assessment and measurement is a developing field, existing tools are continually improving and new tools emerging. Because of the ongoing change in the field and the variation in the type of projects undertaken, there are tools available for almost any project undertaking. The difficulty is narrowing down the list of available tools in order to select the best match.

Before locating the correct tool to use, public administrators should have the answers to the following questions:

- What does the organization want to achieve with this project?
- What type of resources of time, money, and expertise are available to the organization to undertake this project and its assessment?
- Who will be involved in decision-making and implementation of the assessment?
- Does the organization have the desire and the resources to hire an expert consultant when needed?
- Are there other organizations that have completed similar projects?
- Is this undertaking a small project or is the scope of the undertaking holistic and to be applied to all the components of organizational action?
- How will the organization manage ongoing assessment?

The following is a list of suggestions to help administrators select an appropriate tool for sustainable assessment once the above questions are answered:

- Explore tools used by other agencies with similar project undertakings and revise them to meet the organization's needs.
- Consider using classic assessment and decision-making tools of public administration such as strategic planning, cost-benefit analysis, SWOT analysis, and Political, Economic, Social, and Technological analysis (PEST).

- Revise tools that the organization is familiar with to include a sustainability dimension.
- Consult with colleges and universities in the community to locate assessment experts, experienced interns, written information on assessment processes, and completed assessments on similar projects.
- Locate online case studies from credible sources about similar projects.
- Consider hiring a consultant or employee for application of highly technical tools.
- Collaborate with other organizations with a similar project mission in locating applicable tools and case studies.
- Be an informed consumer of decision-making and assessment tools before committing to a specific tool or set of tools.

Questions to Consider

1. What assessment tools does your agency currently use?
2. How can any of your agency's existing tools be modified for sustainable development assessment?
3. What are the primary opportunities and barriers that your agency faces in order to complete assessments in general and sustainable development assessments in particular?

13

The Future of Sustainable Development in Public Administration

This book calls for change to achieve greater environmental sustainability. Who shall lead this change? Hopefully, it will continue to come from all directions. Citizens, grassroots nonprofit organizations, international nongovernmental organizations, businesses, and governments across the world are all involved already. But these groups have differing interests and are hard to bring into a coalition to stimulate change; and even after change is adopted, the real work just begins in interpreting and implementing the policies. The U.S. government does not respond well to comprehensive reform proposals because power is intentionally diffused by institutions of federalism, separation of powers, and bicameralism.

These challenges to sustainability are real, but the potential is great. If this potential is to be realized, public administrators will have to be the midwives of this transformation. Because many different interests and professions are involved in a complex, dispersed network, administrators need to act as go-betweens to implement the policies of sustainability. As Hamilton, writes, "today's public administrator needs to be the epitome of Harlan Cleveland's[1]

---

[1]Harlan Cleveland was an American diplomat and academic. He served as U.S. Ambassador to NATO, President of the University of Hawaii, Dean of the Hubert Humphrey Institute of Public Affairs at the University of Minnesota and the Maxwell School of Citizenship and Public Affairs at Syracuse University.

'get-it-all-together' professional—conversant with a wide variety of fields of study, able to manage multidisciplinary teams, able to draw on a wide range of knowledge to get her/his job done" (2007, 13). These skills are exactly those needed to implement sustainable practices.

Today, public administrators have enormous opportunities to contribute to environmental sustainability and sustainable development decision-making. Every day, more information about creating sustainable communities is added to the knowledge base in public administration. New tools and technologies can be used along with the many tools already available to public administrators. Old tools can also be modified to better match developments in the field and to address the specific needs of communities contributing to the charge for environmentally sustainable communities. The high level of commitment to environmental sustainability in this era provides public administration with the chance to create meaningful actions plans and to lead positive change.

With this growing emphasis on sustainable development, it is important to remember lessons already learned on the journey. Key themes in leading sustainable development in public administration include the following:

- Public administration is well suited for a leadership role in sustainable development because of its boundary-spanning ability and its historic commitment to efficiency, effectiveness, equity, and citizen participation.
- Sustainable development decision-making in public administration is built on the use of citizen time and place knowledge, as well as the technical expertise of professionals.
- Meaningful positive change in sustainable development depends on systems theories approaches to planning.
- Planning for both the short run and the long run is a key responsibility of public administrators practicing sustainable development.
- Measurement and assessment are a necessary component of sound decision-making in sustainable development.
- Collaboration between governments, nonprofit agencies, for-profit agencies, and citizens can lead to better-integrated and more effective sustainable development planning.

The world's communities are increasingly demanding environmentally sustainable goods and services from governments and private organizations. The environment itself is forcing people to pay it more attention as human action impacts the availability and quality of resources. Public administration can and should lead progress toward more sustainable development.

References

ABC News. 2006. Katrina's economic impact: One year later. August. http://abcnews. go.com/Business/HurricaneKatrina/Story?id=2348619&page=4.

Allan, T. 2002. *The Middle East Water Question: Hydropolitics and the Global Economy.* London: I.B. Tauris.

American Lung Association. 2002. *Annotated Bibliography of Recent Studies on the Health Effects of Air Pollution.* New York: American Lung Association.

American Red Cross. 2006. Hurricane season 2005: A season in review. June 30. www. riversidecounty.redcross.org/article.aspx?&a=4165.

Anderson, J.E. 2003. *Public Finance: Principles and Policy.* Boston: Houghton Mifflin.

Association for Commuter Transportation. 2002. *ACT's TEA-21 Platform and Recommendations.* Washington, DC: Association for Commuter Transportation.

Barbier. 1987. The concept of sustainable economic development. *Environmental Conservation* 14 (2): 101–110.

Bartle, J., and D. Leuenberger. 2006. The idea of sustainable development in public administration. *Public Works Management and Policy* 10: 191–194.

Benfield, F.K., and M. Replogle. 2002. The road more traveled: Sustainable transportation in America—or not. *Environmental Law Reporter* 32: 10633–10647.

Black, W.R. 2004. Sustainable transport: Definitions and responses. Paper presented at the TRB/NRC Symposium on Sustainable Transportation. Baltimore, MD.

Bleijenberg, A., and R. Wit. 1998. *Aviation Charge Feasibility Study.* Delft, Netherlands: Centre for Energy Conservation and Environmental Technology.

Bosselman, K. 2001. University and sustainability: Compatible agendas? *Educational Philosophy and Theory* 33 (2): 167–185.

Boucher, D. 1999. *The Paradox of Plenty: Hunger in a Bountiful World.* Oakland, CA: Food First Books.

Brockhagen, D., and M. Lienemeyer. 1999. *Proposal for a European Aviation Charge: Design and Implementation with Respect to International Economical, Ecological, Legal and Political Constraints.* Delft, Netherlands: Centre for Energy Conservation and Environmental Technology.

Bureau of Transportation Statistics (BTS). 2003a. *Transportation Statistics Annual Report.* Washington, DC: Bureau of Transportation Statistics.

———. 2003b. Commuting expenses: Disparity for the working poor. *Issue Brief* 1 (March). www.bts.gov/publications/issue_briefs/number_01/pdf/entire.pdf.

————. 2008. 2007 transportation fatalities by mode. *National Transportation Statistics*. Washington, DC: Bureau of Transportation Statistics. www.bts.gov/publications/national_transportation_statistics/html/table_02_01.html.

Button, K. 2004. Airlines. Presented at the meeting of STELLA/STAR Focus Group 5: Institutions, Regulations and Markets in Transportation. Anavyssos, Greece. www.stellaproject.org.

Carlson, S. 2006. In search of the sustainable campus. *Chronicle of Higher Education* 53 (9): A10.

Chastko, P. 2004. *Alberta's Oil Sands*. Calgary, Canada: University of Calgary Press.

Chase, G. 1998. Faculty development for environmental sustainability in higher education. *Electronic Green Journal*, December.

Chicago Climate Exchange. 2008. www.chicagoclimatex.com.

Childs, K., and R. Croxton. 2005. Human-centered sustainable design. In *Sustainable Architecture White Papers*, ed. Paul Hawken, 39–45. New York: Earth Pledge.

Coase, R.H. 1960. The Problem of Social Cost. *Journal of Law and Economics* 3: 1–44. Coca Cola Company. 2008. Our company. www.thecoca-colacompany.com/ourcompany/index.html.

Conca, K. 2006. *Contentious Transnational Politics and Institution Building*. Cambridge, MA: MIT Press.

Connor, R., and S. Dovers. 2004. *Institutional Change for Sustainable Development*. Cheltenham, UK: Edward Elgar.

Creighton, S.H. 2001. *Greening the Ivory Tower: Improving the Environmental Track Record of Universities, Colleges, and Other Institutions*. Cambridge, MA: MIT Press.

Cropper, M.L., and W. Oates. 1992. Environmental economics: A survey. *Journal of Economic Literature* 30 (2): 675–740.

Davis, S. 1997. *Spectacular Nature, Corporate Culture, and the Sea World Experience*. Berkeley: University of California Press.

Dempsey, P.S. 2000. Trade and transport policy in inclement skies: The conflict between sustainable air transportation and neo-classical economics. *Journal of Air Law and Commerce* 65: 639–693.

Department of Ecology, State of Washington. 2008. Solid waste. www.ecy.wa.gov/programs/swfa/.

Diamond, J. 2004. *Collapse: How societies choose to fail or succeed*. London: Viking Adult.

Dizard, J. 1999. *Going Wild: Hunting, Animals, Rights, and the Contested Meaning of Nature*. Amherst: University of Massachusetts Press.

Dye, T.R. 1992. *Understanding Public Policy*. Englewood Cliffs, NJ: Prentice Hall.

Ellis, R. 2004. *No Turning Back: The Life and Death of Animal Species*. New York: Harper Collins.

Environmental Services Association. 2006. Incineration. September. www.esauk.org/waste/incineration/060927_energy_from_waste.asp.

Ernst, M., J. Corless, and R. Greene-Roesel. 2003. *Clearing the Air: Public Health Threats from Cars and Heavy Duty Vehicles: Why We Need to Protect Federal Clean Air Laws*. Washington, DC: Surface Transportation Policy Project.

Famine Early Warning Systems Network (FEWSNET). 2008. Price watch: Urban food markets in FEWSNET countries. June. http://v4.fews.net/docs/Publications/fews%20net%20monthly%20price%20watch_2008_07_07.pdf.

Gibson, C., M. McKean, and E. Ostrom. 2000. *People and Forests: Communities, Institutions, and Governance*. Boston: MIT Press.

Giddens, A. 2003. *Runaway World*. New York: Routledge.

Glennon, R. 2002. *Water Follies: Groundwater Pumping and the Fate of America's Freshwaters*. Washington, DC: Island Press.

Gramlich, E.M. 1994. Infrastructure investment: A review essay. *Journal of Economic Literature* 32 (3): 1176–1196.

Hall, D. and K. Reeves. 2006. A study of United States hydroelectric plant ownership. www.hydropower.id.doe.gov/hydrofacts/pdfs/a_study_of_united_states_hydroelectric _plant_ownership.pdf.

Hamilton, M.R. 2007. Democracy and public service. In *Democracy and Public Administration*, ed. R.C. Box. Armonk, NY: M.E. Sharpe.

Hanson, E. 2002. *Animal Attractions: Nature on Display in American Zoos.* Princeton: Princeton University Press.

Hardin, G. 1968. The tragedy of the commons. *Science*, December 13, 1243–1248.

Hawken, P., A. Lovins, and L.H. Lovins. 1999. *Natural Capitalism: Creating the Next Industrial Revolution.* Boston: Little, Brown.

Heinberg, R. 2000. *The Oil Depletion Protocol.* Gabriola Island, Canada: New Society.

Hewlett-Packard. 2008. Global citizenship. www.hp.com/hpinfo/globalcitizenship /environment/envprogram/index.html.

HMFH. Architects and Vermont Energy Investment Corp. 2005. The incremental costs and benefits of green schools in Massachusetts. December 19. www.masstech.org /renewableenergy/green_schools/HMFHstudy121905.pdf.

Horan, T.A., H. Dittmar, and D.R. Jordan. 1999. ISTEA and the new era in transportation policy: Sustainable communities from a federal initiative. In *Toward Sustainable Communities: Transition and Transformations in Environmental Policy*, ed. D.A. Mazmanian and M.E. Kraft, 217–245. Cambridge, MA: MIT Press.

IBM. 2008. Environment. www.ibm.com/ibm/environment/.

The International Union for Conservation of Nature (IUCN). 2008. Members' database. http://cms.iucn.org/about/union/members/network/members_database/index.cfm.

Kats, G., and Capital E. 2003. The costs and financial benefits of green buildings: A report to California's sustainable building task force. October. www.ciwmb.ca.gov /greenbuilding/Design/CostBenefitReport.pdf.

———. 2006. Greening America's schools: Costs and benefits. October. www.cap-e.com /ewebeditpro/items/O59F9819.pdf.

Kennedy-Glans, D., and B. Schulz. 2005. *Corporate Integrity: A Tool Kit for Managing Beyond Compliance.* Ontario, Canada: John Wiley.

Khagram, S. 2004. *Dams and Development: Transnational Struggles for Water and Power.* Ithaca, NY: Cornell University Press.

King County, State of Washington. 2008. King County: Environmentally preferable lubricants. www.metrokc.gov/procure/green/oil.htm.

Lappe, F.M., J. Collins, and P. Rosset. 1998. *World Hunger: 12 Myths.* New York: Grove Press.

Leone, R.A. 1999. Technology-forcing public policies and the automobile. In *Essays in Transportation Economics and Policy: A Handbook in Honor of John R. Meyer*, ed. J.A. Gómez-Ibáñez, W.B. Tye, and C. Winston, 291–324. Washington, DC: Brookings Institution Press.

Leuenberger, D. 2006. Sustainable development in public administration: A match with practice? *Public Works Management and Policy* 10 (3): 195–201.

Leuenberger, D., and M. Wakin. 2007. Sustainable development in public administration planning: An exploration of social justice, equity, and citizen inclusion. *Administrative Theory and Praxis* 29 (3): 370–374.

Martin, L.L., and P.M. Kettner. 1996. *Measuring the Performance of Human Service Programs.* Thousand Oaks, CA: Sage.

Massachusetts Sustainable Design Roundtable. Chap. 11, p. 4, 2006.

Mazmanian, D.A., and M.E. Kraft. 2001. *Toward Sustainable Communities: Transition and Transformations in Environmental Policy.* Cambridge, MA: MIT Press.

Miller, P., and J. Moffet. 1993. *The Price of Mobility: Uncovering the Hidden Costs of Transportation.* New York: Natural Resources Defense Council.

National Audubon Society. 2008. Mission statement. www.audubon.org/nas/about.html.

National Research Council (NRC). 1998. *Atmospheric Change and the North American Transportation Sector: Summary of a Trilateral Workshop.* Washington, DC: National Research Council.

———. 2003. *For Greener Skies: Reducing Environmental Impacts of Aviation.* Washington, DC: National Academy Press.

National Resource Defense Council. 2008. Mission statement. www.nrdc.org/about/.

Nicholson, W., and C. Snyder. 2007. *Intermediate Microeconomics and Its Applications.* 10th ed. Mason, OH: Thomson South-Western.

Nord, M., M. Andrews, and S. Carlson. 2007. Household food security in the United States, 2006. Economic Research Report No. ERR-49, November. www.ers.usda.gov /Publications/ERR49/.

O'Connell, B. 1999. *Civil Society: The Underpinnings of American Democracy.* Hanover, NH: University Press of New England.

Okun, Arthur M. 1975. *Equality and Efficiency: The Big Tradeoff.* Washington, DC: Brookings Institution Press.

Ostrom, E. 1990. *Governing the Commons: The Evolution of Institutions for Collective Action.* London: Cambridge University Press.

Ostrom, E., L. Schroeder, and S. Wynne. 1993. *Institutional Incentives and Sustainable Development: Infrastructure Policies in Perspective.* Boulder, CO: Westview Press.

Payne, P.G. 2006. Environmental education and curriculum theory. *Journal of Environmental Education* 37 (2): 25–33.

Pearce, D.W., A. Markandya, and E.B. Barbier. 1989. *Blueprint for a Green Economy.* London: Earthscan.

Pearson, S., S. Honeywood, and M. O'Toole. 2005. Not yet learning for sustainability: The challenge of environmental education in a university. *International Research in Geographical and Environmental Education* 14 (3): 173–184.

Pigou, A.C. 1946. *The Economics of Welfare.* 4th ed. London: Macmillan.

Postel, S. 1999. *Pillar of Sand: Can the Irrigation Miracle Last?* New York: W.W. Norton.

Ralston, K., C. Newman, A. Clauson, J. Guthrie, and J. Buzby. 2008. The National School Lunch Program: Background, trends, and issues. Economic Research Report No. ERR-61, July. www.ers.usda.gov/Publications/ERR61/.

Reid, A., and P. Petocz. 2006. University lecturers' understanding of sustainability. *Higher Education* 51 (1): 105–123.

Ringius, L. 2001. *Radioactive Waste Disposal at Sea: Public Ideas, Transnational Policy Entrepreneurs, and Environmental Regimes.* Boston: MIT Press.

Ritzer, G. 2008. *The McDonaldization of Society.* Thousand Oaks, CA: Pine Forge Press.

Rogers, H. 2005. *Gone Tomorrow: The Hidden Life of Garbage.* New York: W.W. Norton.

Rogers, P.P., K.F. Jalal, and J.A. Boyd. 2006. *An Introduction to Sustainable Development.* Cambridge, MA: Harvard University Press.

Roots and Shoots. 2008. Mission statement. www.rootsandshoots.org/aboutus /mission.

Roseland, M., S. Connelly, D. Hendrickson, C. Lindberg, and M. Lithgrow. 2005. *Toward sustainable communities.* Gabriola Island, Canada: New Society Publishers.

Rothfeder, J. 2001. *Every Drop for Sale.* New York: Penguin Books.

Sabatier, P., W. Focht, M. Lubell, Z. Trachtenberg, A. Vedlitz, and M. Matlock. 2005. *Swimming Upstream: Collaborative Approaches to Watershed Management.* Cambridge, MA: MIT Press.

Savas, E.S. 2000. *Privatization and Public-Private Partnerships.* New York: Seven Bridges Press.

Schafer, A., and D. Victor. 1997. The past and future of global mobility. *Scientific American,* October, 58.

Schweppe, E. 2001. Legacy of a landmark: ISTEA after 10 years. *Public Roads* 65 (3): 2–6.

Shapland, G. 1997. *Rivers of Discord: International Water Disputes in the Middle East.* New York: St. Martin's Press.

Shiva, V. 1992. *The Violence of the Green Revolution: Third World Agriculture, Ecology, and Politics.* New York: St. Martin's Press.

———. 1999. *Biopiracy: The Plunder of Nature and Knowledge.* Boston: South End Press.

———. 2000. *Stolen Harvest: The Hijacking of the Global Food Supply.* Cambridge, MA: South End Press.

Simon, H.A. 1946 The proverbs of public administration. In *The Classics of Public Administration,* 3rd ed. (pp. 150–166) ed. M. Shafritz and A.C. Hyde. Fort Worth: Harcourt Brace.

Simonsen, W., and M. Robbins. 2000. *Citizen Participation in Resource Allocation.* Boulder, CO: Westview Press.

Small, K.A. 1992. Using the revenues from congestion pricing. *Transportation* 19 (4): 359–381.

Small, K.A., C. Winston, and C.A. Evans. 1989. *Road Work: A New Highway Pricing and Investment Policy.* Washington, DC: Brookings Institution Press.

Smith, A. 1909. *An Inquiry into the Nature and Causes of the Wealth of Nations,* ed. C.J. Bullock (Harvard Classics). New York: Collier Press.

Stone, C. 1974. *Should Trees Have Standing? Toward Legal Rights for Natural Objects.* Los Altos, CA: William Kaufmann.

Stough, R.R., and P. Rietveld. 2005. Institutional dimensions of sustainable transport. In *Barriers to Sustainable Transport: Institutions, Regulation, and Sustainability,* ed. P. Rietveld. London: Routledge.

Svara, J., and J. Brunet. 2004. Filling in the skeletal pillar: Addressing social equity in introductory courses in public administration. *Journal of Public Affairs Education.* 10: 99–109.

Swan, S.H., and B. Vaitca. 2007. *The Justice of Eating: The Struggle for Food and Dignity in Recent Humanitarian Crises.* Northampton, UK: Pluto Press.

Toyota. 2008. Vision. www.toyota.co.jp/en/vision/sustainability/index.html.

Transport for London. 2007. *Central London Congestion Charging: Impacts Monitoring.* Fifth Annual Report. London: Transport for London.

Truett, R. 2004. Cost, reliability issues delay fuel cell use. *Automotive News,* October 18, 32.

Ubbels, B., and E. Verhoef. 2005. Barriers to Transport Pricing. *In Barriers to Sustainable Transport: Institutions, Regulation and Sustainability,* ed. P. Rietveld and R.R. Stough. New York: Spon Press.

United Kingdom Royal Commission on Environmental Pollution. 1994. *Transport and the Environment.* London: Royal Commission on Environmental Pollution.

United Nations Economic and Social Commission for Asia and the Pacific (UNESCAP), and Asian Institute of Transport Development. 2001. *Sustainable Transport Pricing and Charges: Principles and Issues* (ST/ESCAP/2139). www.unescap.org/ttdw /Publications/TPTS_pubs/pricing_fulltext.pdf.

United Nations World Food Program. 2008. WFP interactive map. www.wfp.org/country _brief/hunger_map/map/hungermap_popup/map_popup.html.

U.S. Department of Agriculture (USDA), Economic Research Service. 2008a. Foodborne illness cost calculator. www.ers.usda.gov/data/Foodborneillness/.

————. 2008b. Wheat data: Yearbook tables. www.ers.usda.gov/Data/Wheat /WheatYearbook.aspx#WorldSD.

U.S. Department of Energy. 2008. Hydropower. www.doe.gov/energysources /hydropower.htm.

U.S. Environmental Protection Agency (EPA). 2008a. Municipal solid waste generation, recycling, and disposal in the United States. www.epa.gov/epaoswer/non-hw/muncpl /pubs/msw06.pdf.

————. 2008b. Wastes—non-hazardous waste—municipal solid waste: Landfills. www .epa.gov/osw/nonhaz/municipal/landfill.htm.

————. 2008c. Municipal solid waste commodities. www.epa.gov/epaoswer/non-hw /muncpl/comm.htm.

Von Hayek, Friedrich A. 1945. The use of knowledge in society. *American Economic Review* 35 (4): 519–530.

Wachs, M. 2003. Improving efficiency and equity in transportation finance. *Brookings Institution Series on Transportation Reform*, April, 1–19.

————. 2004. What are the challenges to creating a sustainable transportation? How can transportation systems become more sustainable? Paper presented at the TRB/NRC Symposium on Sustainable Transportation. Baltimore, MD.

Wal-Mart Stores. 2008, Global IWM Stores. www.walmartstores.com /GlobalWMStoresWeb.

The Walt Disney Company. 2008. Environmentality. www. corporate.disney.go.com /environmentality/marketing.html.

Ward, D.P. 2002.*Water Wars: Drought, Flood, Folly, and the Politics of Thirst.* New York: Berkley Publishing Group.

Weaver, J.H., M.T. Rock, and K. Kusterer. 1997. *Achieving Broad-Based Sustainable Development: Governance, Environment, and Growth with Equity.* West Hartford, CT: Kumarian Press.

Whitelegg, J., and H. Cambridge. 2004. Aviation and sustainability: A policy paper. Stockholm, Sweden: Stockholm Environmental Institute.

Wikipedia. 2008. Chicago climate exchange. http://en.wikipedia.org/wiki/Chicago _Climate_Exchange.

Winfrey, J.C. 1998. *Social Issues: The Ethics and Economics of Taxes and Public Programs.* New York: Oxford University Press.

Winston, C. 2006. *Government Failure versus Market Failure: Microeconomics Policy Research and Government Performance.* Washington: AEI-Brookings Joint Center for Regulatory Studies.

Wise, S. 2002. *Drawing the Line: Science and the Case for Animal Rights.* Cambridge, MA: Perseus Books.

Woods Hole Research Center. 2008. Mission statement. www.whrc.org/about_us /mission.htm.

World Bank. 2008a. Cambodia: Rehabilitating the urban water sector. http://go.worldbank .org/A3IF6BF9K0.

REFERENCES

———. 2008b. Colombia: Local solutions improve water and sanitation services. http://go.worldbank.org/R6TL0XWCB0.

World Business Council for Sustainable Development (WBCSD). 2004. Mobility 2030: Meeting the challenges to sustainability. July 5. www.wbcsd.org/plugins/DocSearch/details.asp?type=DocDet&ObjectId=6094.

World Wildlife Fund. 2008. Mission statement. www.worldwildlife.org/who/index.html.

Index

About the Authors

Deniz Zeynep Leuenberger is Associate Professor of Political Science and Public Administration and Faculty Director of the Institute for Regional Development at Bridgewater State College in Bridgewater, Massachusetts. She received her MPA and PhD from the University of Nebraska at Omaha. Her mission is to provide citizens and public, nonprofit, and nongovernmental agency leaders with tools to increase community environmental sustainability, to improve resource use efficiency, and to integrate outcomes measurement in decision making. Dr. Leuenberger specializes in sustainable development, public sector economics, public budgeting and finance, and nonprofit and nongovernmental organization management. She is especially interested in the use of sustainable development and strategic planning in public and nonprofit organizations in the United States of America, the European Union, and the Middle East and North Africa. She also has developed several community-based projects that focus on citizen education and sustainable development in southeastern Massachusetts and in New England. She has published articles on sustainable development in publications such as *Administrative Theory and Praxis*, *Public Works Management & Policy*, *State and Local Government Review*, *PA Times*, and *Public Manager.* She has worked in health and human services administration in government and nonprofit organizations.

John R. Bartle is the David Scott Diamond Professor of Public Affairs and Director of the School of Public Administration at the University of Nebraska at Omaha, as well as part-time research fellow and visiting professor at the Center for Public Administration, Sun Yat-sen University, Guangzhou, China. He is the editor of *Evolving Theories of Public Budgeting* (2001) and of several articles in journals such as *Public Administration Review*, *Journal of Public*

Administration Research and Theory, *Public Budgeting & Finance*, *Public Works Management & Policy*, and *State and Local Government Review.* Dr. Bartle is a member of the Executive Council of the National Association of Schools of Public Affairs and Administration, past chair of the Association for Budgeting and Financial Management, and a former member of the National Council of the American Society for Public Administration. He holds a BA (honors) in economics from Swarthmore College, an MPA from the University of Texas at Austin, and a PhD from the School of Public Policy and Management at Ohio State University. He has worked in city and state government in Minnesota and for state and national nonprofit research organizations on tax policy issues.